Not Afraid

Stories of Confronting Fear

Edited by Alise Wright

NOT AFRAID

ISBN # 978-0615896540
Published by Civitas Press, LLC
San Jose, CA,
www.civitaspress.com

Not Afraid

Stories of Confronting Fear

Edited by Alise Wright

CivitasPress
Publishing inspiring and redemptive ideas.[sm]

Dedication

To those who find the courage to confront their fear.

Contents

Fear and Your Relationships

Preface

In September of 2011, we published the community project *Not Alone, Stories of Living with Depression*, edited by a talented author Alise Wright. She had gathered together a unique set of voices willing to openly share their experiences with depression. It was a wonderful work of shear talent and courage. The book received rave reviews and gave people with depression a voice.

As Alise and I discussed the possibility of another project, one thing continually rose to the surface: confronting fear. *Not Alone* was essentially stories of people confronting their fear by sharing their experience with depression. But what if we opened the idea up to include people dealing with other topics, like relationships, faith, and work. It was a great idea. The work you are about to read is the culmination of that idea.

As you read these stories, allow yourself the real opportunity to consider one significant idea. What would happen if you, too, were not afraid? What would happen if you confronted my fear? Would your life be forever changed? As these stories attest, the answer is unequivocally yes.

As with all Community projects, and because of the nature of the content, we've chosen not to edit for language, and in some cases for grammar. We wanted to maintain the distinctive voice and thought process of each writer. Our hope is that in these pages you would begin to share in the experience of what it means to be human. Sometimes it's not pretty. Sometimes it's downright ugly. But in the midst of this suffering, we learn that we can overcome, that we are worth it, and that we can continue.

Much love

Jonathan Brink, Publisher

Fear and Your Profession

Introduction

By Alise Wright

I found freedom from fear thanks to Neil Diamond's "Sweet Caroline."

For as long as I can remember, music has been a part of my life. I had been singing in my church and with my family since my very earliest days, and had been playing the piano since I started lessons in third grade. In college, I abandoned my early thoughts of studying communications to instead pursue a degree in music education. Music was my everything.

My heart beats for music. When I play, I feel like I am connecting with the Divine. It might be a playful expression. It might be a soulful expression. It might even be an angry expression. But regardless of how it is put forth, when I play, I am treading on holy ground with a sacred friend.

Music can be a cruel soul-mate. I received life and beauty and redemption from her, but she was also the place of my deepest wounding.

Not everything negative about music is automatically a wounding. There were performances that didn't go quite as well as I hoped they would. Auditions that didn't turn out in my favor. Critical comments from teachers and peers.

Most of these things were fine. I could use them to become a better musician. I was able to look past the small hurt that it caused in the moment and see the big picture of how I could improve my craft despite that disappointment.

But there were some wounds that went much deeper. Rather than focusing on things like mechanics and technique, these were critical of my heart. Not enough passion, too much focus on self, no genuine love present. They went into that holy space that I found when playing and desecrated it.

Each time this happened, a piece of the joy that I found in music was replaced with fear. Fear that I wasn't as talented as I thought that I was. Fear that I would never have a career doing something that I loved. Fear that my motives were tainted, and that the pure love that I felt for music wasn't as pure as I believed.

In 2006, the final shred of joy that I found in music was gone. The church where I had been playing and leading worship had abandoned me and told me that I could not have anything to do with music ministry, despite specifically recruiting me for the position. It was the most painful blow that I had received and while I had said that I would never abandon music when this happened, I would not play again for nearly a year and a half.

As time passed, I slowly found my way back to music. I sang for the children in our church. I began filling in occasionally on the church worship team. The door to holiness found through music began to crack open, just a sliver.

Finally, one of the members of the worship team asked if I would fill in for his regular keyboard player in his cover band. I was hesitant to accept, because there was so much music to learn and I was still overcoming the voices that screamed in my head that I wasn't good enough. But it paid and I thought that it might be fun, so did my best to block out the negative voices and said yes. Yes to cheesy songs, yes to a book full of music I didn't have time to memorize, yes to a group of people that I didn't know very well, yes to a job that I thought I might actually enjoy.

That yes didn't change everything right away. After my first rehearsal, I was so riddled with insecurity that I came home and sobbed because I didn't know how to play the opening part of Sweet Caroline and I was sure that I was going to ruin the entire wedding reception with my incompetence.

But I made it through that performance. And the next and the next. And as I continued to play, I found that I was once again having fun. That music was once again becoming a place where I could find joy and excitement and happiness, rather than being an area that was just buried in fear.

This transformation continued and as it did, I found that fear fell off of other places in my professional life. I began to get serious about writing and publishing when I had only been playing at it for years. I began teaching piano lessons. The rumblings of that one yes to learning a cheesy Neil Diamond song became an avalanche of yeses to opportunities that presented themselves. Rather than simply ignoring these moments, I began to view them as positions that I could pursue. Positions at which I could succeed.

In this section of the book, the authors give us a glimpse into the choices that they had to make in order to overcome fear in their professional lives. Sonny needed to overcome his fear of being seen as unworthy of a leadership position in his church. You will read of Kathy's decision to face her fears about leaving her family behind as she followed her calling to become a pastor. In his essay, Rich shares how he had to address both fear of his family of origin and potential failure as a provider for his family when he chose to follow his dreams rather than the practical path.

One of the first questions that we're often asked when we meet someone new is, "What do you do?" Answering that question without fear or shame is a gift and in the following stories, you will read of people who have chosen to embrace their professions without that fear.

1

Something New

By Melody Harrison Hanson

Often, I wrestle with God. I am a doubter.
Though I regret my own suspicions and fear,
I am also strangely grateful.
Yes, I am glad for to wrestle is honest.
And I have seen as I face my darkest hours,
as twilight turns to morning and I am still awake,
as I fight and the agony of depression and anxiety overwhelm.

God is my comfort.
Even as I battle, I know his consolation.
All this comes, unsurprisingly, *for me*.
Somehow I know with the albatross of fear hanging heavy and
when the arrows of anxiety are stabbing in my chest,
I know.

God is God. And I am simply and solely, wholly and fully,
unabashedly His *beloved*.
Oh, I may plead with God shouting "Bless Me!"
But I understand its slow coming

and my slow learning
that *even here,* now, today I am already blessed.
I may walk through life with this fear and sorrow.
Scars deep, for I have been wounded.
I will cry out begging God to prove himself to me.
Does he mean for my life to mean anything?

Can I trust?

Can I count on you for whatever the future holds?
Trust that my life matters?
I know these encounters in the dark, the isolation
and despair *change me.*

Deep within, through my abrasions and soul pain,
God is making something *new.*
I bear the mark of my pain in scars upon my soul.
But I am also something *else, something good.*
Therein is any confidence,
hope. I am someone redeemed.

So even while I stumble, shattered
I am being made strong – perhaps even useful, resolute
And yes, somehow my life is something good.
Then I can believe when God made me he was pleased.
And nothing I can do, have done, will ever do changes that.

Deep within my abrasions and soul pain, the God who made me
is making me into something new.

2

Doing Hard Things Scared

By Kathy Escobar

It was a few hours before my kids got home from school. I was in a whirlwind, finishing as much as I could before they filled the house with a trail of homework, backpacks, and messy snacks. My cell phone rang. I didn't recognize the number, but I answered it anyway. The call was from an old friend from our past church, and it felt weird that he'd be calling me since we rarely talked. He said he knew I was at Denver Seminary and "was looking to hire a care pastor for his growing church."

"Um, I can't think of anyone off the top of my head," I replied, "but let me think about it and I'll let you know if anyone comes to mind."

"Well, actually, I wasn't calling to network. I was calling to see if you were interested in the job."

I immediately sank onto my dirty kitchen floor, my head learning against the cupboard, thinking, "What? Did I just hear him correctly?"

I caught my breath and mumbled, "Did you just say you were asking me?"

"Yes, I know the work you've been doing, and I think you're the right person for it."

I'll never forget that moment, now nine years ago, when somebody first believed in my work enough to actually pay for it. For many years I was a solid volunteer leader at various churches we attended, serving dutifully and helping other people, but never with the feeling of being strongly valued.

We set up a lunch meeting. I pulled myself together, trying to pretend I wasn't as excited as I actually was about the opportunity. This role had it all--healing community, recovery, pastoral care, spiritual direction, and teaching. These were all the things I loved to do. Above all, the ministry was centered on what was most important to me—relationship.

I left the meeting excited, exuberant. Here was an opportunity handed to me on a silver platter, with a flexible schedule, a chance to shape a ministry from the ground up, and good money to boot. When I got home, I shared enthusiastically with Jose, my husband and father of my five children, then ranging in age from 3 to 11 years old.

His first words in response: "I thought you weren't going to go back to work until the twins were in kindergarten." Immediately, all the hope and excitement I felt quickly deflated. He was right. I had made that commitment when we first had kids, but the twins were a surprise, for goodness sake, our fourth and fifth children; was he really going to still hold me to that vow? I had been home with little kids for 11 straight years. Eleven years of naps, snacks, library hours, play dates, and putting myself on the back burner so that they could be on front.

Anger rose inside of me as he sat waiting for my response. I had expected he'd be just as excited as I was. His reaction fueled resentment in my heart, and I could feel my blood boiling just below the surface. Even though my insides were fuming, on the outside I gritted my teeth, nodded my head, and responded with a defeated, "I guess you're right."

In that moment, I was terrified to step into my desire and say what I really wanted. I was paralyzed with fear of what it would really mean to say, "I want this enough to fight for it."

Over the following weeks, we talked to a few other close friends, and much to my surprise most of them agreed with Jose. That made me even angrier. The timing just wasn't right, they said. They were scared for me, juggling work and kids. Their fear blotted out any courage that I tried to muster.

After a few weeks of realizing this just wasn't going to happen, I took a deep breath and dialed my friend's number. "I'm sorry, but I just can't go to work quite yet. Thanks for thinking of me." When I hung up the phone, I bawled my head off and wanted to throw up.

Why couldn't I fight for what I wanted?

Why couldn't I say what I was really feeling?

Why couldn't I disagree with my husband and my friends?

Fear.

It's that simple. I was afraid to want something. I was afraid to go against others' approval. I was afraid to rock the boat.

For a year, I silently grieved my decision and pretended it didn't really bother me as much as it did (I'm really good at that). I figured out a way to cope with the loss, amplifying my mommy skills and starting a new ministry at the church we were going to at the time.

About six months after the original call, I had a mini-meltdown at a conference I attended with my husband. I could not stop crying. The six months of stuffing my disappointment came out in a flood.

The tears and grief overwhelmed me, and I knew in that moment this situation was so much more than missing out on a job opportunity.

It was about killing off my desire for the sake of the status quo.

It was about not being honest with my husband and friends about how deeply I wanted to be part of something bigger.

It was about the painful realization that I hadn't even prayed for help or asked God for input or direction; the little resistance I felt in the beginning was enough for me to lay it down and pretend it didn't matter.

It was about being paralyzed by fear instead of being willing to do some hard things scared.

My husband held me as I sobbed, and I shared what was really going on for me. I let it all out this time, not holding back. I shared my resentment, fear, anger, and the crazy thoughts that were swirling around in my head. He listened. He didn't offer advice or try to fix it. He was amazing in that moment. He held me and said, "I am so sorry; I honestly didn't realize what a big deal this was for you, and I was just afraid, too."

Six more months passed. I still cried now and then, but so much relief came through the honesty of owning my fears and sharing them with Jose and our friends.

Almost exactly one year later, I received a voice mail from my friend. "We never hired anybody. It's a long story, but I'm calling you again to see if maybe this time you'll say yes."

That moment was surreal. After finally letting it go, this opportunity was somehow back in my hands. When I told my husband about the call, he laughed and said, "This time, there's no way I'm saying no. Let's walk through the process and see what happens."

It would be easy to think it would be a relief, but the truth is that fear once again swept in. I felt afraid to open my heart again to the possibility.

I walked through the process more honestly this second time around.

I said out loud how excited but how scared I was. I let myself want it. I let myself fight for it. I let myself line up all the reasons it didn't make sense but I should do it anyway. I let myself give up the vow I should have never made in the first place about waiting until the kids were in kindergarten and figured out an easy daycare situation for them a few short hours a week. I let myself not know how it was all going to really work out.

I let myself say "yes."

And I prayed for courage, which I think is best defined as "doing hard things scared."

With hands shaking and my heart beating fast, I finally called my friend and said, "I'm in. I'm scared, but I'm in."

My yes did not start everything rolling downhill. In fact, the next two years were two of the most uphill, brutal years of my life in many ways. Through the ups and downs of this ministry position, my integrity was tested, my marriage was challenged, and my faith was rocked. Each day I prayed for courage to not give up, to embrace the fire God ignited in me to pastor and lead. But no matter how clear it felt that I was supposed to be there, almost every day I had to reckon with my choice and the feelings inside of not being good enough as a pastor, wife, and working mother.

But what had shifted in me was a resolve that I didn't have before I said yes, a passion that propelled me to keep walking this direction, knowing that courage doesn't mean not having fear. It means doing hard things scared.

3

Success and Failure Are Halves Of A Whole

By Joy Wilson

Most of my life, success and failure have been Siamese twins – different bodies with the same heart. Believing that failure was a given, I have often sabotaged success because I knew I would lose it. I perceived myself as a failure, and lived it. Dreams were something I had while asleep, detached from reality. Other people had dreams of becoming something, someday. I knew better, so kept my dreams tucked in bed.

The one thing I've always known is I'm a good writer. Poetry has been my outlet where it was safe to tell the truth. Through writing, I expressed my fears, doubt, and pain, protecting me from criticism and rejection because nobody knew. Here was a release, a safety valve that kept me sane. I was shielded from an angry God by writing what I couldn't pray. I could scream at those who hurt me, and chronicle despair that my life would ever improve.

Honing my craft as a wordsmith over the years, I knew my work was good and deep down, wished I could share it with those who might understand and affirm my gift. But I couldn't take the risk of their shock at my honesty or distain for the depression that permeates so much of my writing. Why invite attack of my vulnerable heart on the possibility of praise?

So I succeeded in silence, with a fictional audience who acclaimed such audacity. My own private public was me.

I lamented lost loves, blasted bosses, confronted fear. I was brave and powerful on paper. Wars were won, promotions gained, and I could say "fuck you" to God and get away with it. My writing loved me as I was, and we admired each other. But I denied the dream of being published, because why bother with something you can't have? Yeah, but what if? Come on, Joy – Cinderella was a fairytale.

There were genuine outward successes. As an honors student, I wrote an intellectual poem that won Best Poem of the Year in a scholastic contest. Those kinds of poems I let people see: cultural commentaries or witty satire. I was able to obtain praise based on pretense.

Writing went verbal in college, culminating in a Speech Communications degree, and I majored in English Literature during graduate school. One class away from graduating with a Master's degree, I dropped out of school, too threatened by success. So I got jobs without careers, always projecting a professional image. But the real me stayed hidden in notebooks full of poems.

After several disastrous marriages, God brought a wonderful man into my life. Bud and I have been married twelve years now, and I let him read what I write, but no one else. Then that changed through a series of events that only God could arrange.

We have a mutual friend named Connie – one of the least threatening people I know. One day Bud said, "Why don't you share some of your work with Connie?" I felt nervous and shy, but agreed to do it. We went to see her, and I took three or four poems. I wanted to see her reaction.

She was sitting across from me, and when I finished reading a particularly raw, painful poem, Connie fell out of her chair on her knees, laid her head in my lap, and sobbed. Bud and I were shocked. Finally she looked up and said, "I'm in charge of the logistics for a conference two weeks from now. The attendees are non-traditional Christians, many of whom have been marginalized by the Church. I want you to read several of your poems, starting with this one." I froze in terror, screaming "NO!" without words. But another voice in me whispered, "Do it. This is a group of Christian misfits. If anyone will accept my work, it might be this bunch."

When the time came, Bud said he was sure I was going to back out, but I went to the podium, holding my radical writing in trembling hands. "Let's get this over with," I thought. I knew they would be horrified, politely applaud, and then crucify me later. Instead, I received a standing ovation. Many in the crowd had tears streaming down their faces, and hugged me afterwards.

That was shock number one.

Then something happened that changed my life forever. A stranger walked up to me and asked, "Are you published?" No. "How many of these do you have?" About 500. "Where are they?" In a drawer. Without hesitation, he said, "I'm a publisher, and I'm going to publish your work. It's redemptive, and people need to know it's OK to be that honest with God." Seven months later, my book was for sale at Amazon.com and Barnes & Noble.com – *Uncensored Prayer: The Spiritual Practice of Wrestling With God.*

But this story isn't about realizing my dream of having a published book. The most important thing is I took the risk to be real in front of those who hear me speak and read my words. I still battle depression and doubt, but I've learned I can face my fears and survive.

Through God's intervention, I was able to reveal unedited truth, knowing some people will criticize. No one could make this decision for me. I chose to bring my heart out of hiding, gamble with failure, and see if I could handle success based on honesty. Here's what I found:

Heart Hope

Listen to your heart, not your fear.
The heart hears hope
while fear tells lies,
sees spies in even faithful friends
who care enough to ask the second time
how you really are behind the social "Fine,"
whereas heart will help you know the truth
and bear it, if it causes pain,
sustains through boredom and defeat
and lasts to love in spite of fear
that "ifs" and "shoulds" and questions faith,
believing only in disaster,
scoffs at intuition and invalidates experience.

But heart knows what it knows
without need to prove or understand.
When honored, it will tell us
who we are and what we need;
when followed, it will take us home

nose to the ground,
tracking the unseen sacred path
unique to every soul
undeterred by howling in the dark
from terrors without teeth.

4

Providing the Cool

By Rich Chaffins

When I was a young boy, my cousin Doug seemed awesome. Why was he cool? Because he had recently graduated from college, and just opened his own accounting firm in downtown Atlanta. The very apex of cool, right? Yeah, I didn't think so either. But my family sure did. To a coal mining family in southern West Virginia, Doug was a shining light. He was one that got out, and made something of himself. His own firm meant financial security. An upstanding place in society. Doing the right thing. The American Dream™.

I heard a steady stream about Doug, and accounting, from the tender age of 9, on through high school. He came up in every conversation I had at home concerning what I wanted to do with myself in college and beyond. All. The. Time. "Don't you want to have your own business?" "Look at this picture of the new house Doug is building! Isn't it BIG? You want one of those when you're his age, don't you?" I have to admit, up through middle school, I thought that those things were, in fact, pretty cool. Money? Good. More video games. Big house? Rad. I could put a wrestling ring right in the living room.

However, when I was just getting into high school I encountered something that changed all that forever. I would never be the same. I was irrevocably altered.

And what, you ask, could cause such upheaval? What could alter a young man's course so irrefutably? What could warrant such fairly large descriptors?

It most likely won't be surprising to anyone who's seen it, but.... Poison's video for "Nothing But A Good Time", the first single off of their second album. The pyrotechnics. The attitude. The various shades of neon...well...*everything*. The dozen or so different electric guitars C.C. used in the video. Oh, the guitars...the guitars. They looked to me like magic wands, battle axes, and divining rods of unadulterated awesomeness all rolled into one. The imperative instilled itself into my mind: ***I must acquire one of these. I must learn to play it. I must shred, bang my head, and waggle my tongue before the sweaty throngs.***

To my family's dismay, most of my time in high school was taken up playing the crappy electric guitar I had bought. And then the slightly less crappy second guitar. Then the good guitar. Then the guitar that sucked, but looked like a medieval torture device, so it was awesome. With this amazing instrument filling my head at all hours of the day, accounting all of a sudden seemed like slow suicide. I had to do *this* for a living.

Pleading my case to major in music in college before my coal miner family went just like you think it would. Reasoning, pleading, disgust, both from me and my family. They told me that music just wasn't a feasible way to support myself, not to mention my future wife and children. It was too reliant on chance. It wasn't stable enough. In the end, however, I won. I was going to attend West Virginia University, and I was going to major in Guitar Performance, with an emphasis on jazz studies.

Life as a music major is great, provided you're ready for the challenge. Twenty-plus credit hours every semester (31 was my personal best). A minimum of 4 hours a day on your instrument, not counting ensemble rehearsals. In other words, I lived in the music department. Just like all the other music, art, and drama majors. It bears emphasis here that the creative arts programs are designed to weed out the people who don't *need* to be in their chosen field. Many people *think* they want to play an instrument, or paint, or act for a living, but in most cases, only the ones whose sanity relies on doing what they were created to do persevere. I was one of those, and when I left college, I had my music career in front of me. Gigs were lining up. The future looked *amazing.*

Then my girlfriend and I experienced an unplanned pregnancy right before I was supposed to leave for a cruise ship gig. Her due date, in fact, was the day my contract with the cruise company was supposed to end.

And there it was then I thought my dream ended.

I was in turmoil. I couldn't take her with me on a several-month-long cruise ship gig. And I couldn't leave her to deal with making a person, unmarried, while I sailed blithely off into the Caribbean. The fear started to creep in while I tried to sort this out. Maybe I had made a mistake pursuing music. I wasn't sure of anything anymore. So, what did I do?

I decided my family had been right.

I couldn't support my new bride and forthcoming child while being away all the time. I couldn't take my pregnant wife to nightclubs when I played. I couldn't be a real man and a musician.

So I threw in the towel. Put up my guitars, tossed my dream into the back of the closet, and got a 'real' job. Went to work managing restaurants, a job I always told myself I'd never take. Worked the 45-hour weeks. Told myself repeatedly that this was the right thing to do. I should have listened to my family when they told me that my idea of a good life wouldn't work. Maybe if I had, I would've majored in something that would have gotten me the big house. My own business. Maybe even an accounting firm. I tried telling myself that the empty hole in my life was just regret for being so foolish in the first place. That my constant fear of living the rest of my life in this colorless, two-dimensional way was ridiculous.

After a few years of this, we moved back to West Virginia, having spent the first few years of our married life in North Carolina. Misty was homesick, and I thought a change of scenery might help me feel better about not doing what I knew I was made to do. We looked for the church we had gone to while dating, and found it much bigger, and in a different part of town. We went one Sunday, and loved it. We decided to go back the next Sunday.

It was the second time we attended that they announced they were putting together a second worship band to start a rotation, and were holding auditions.

My heart *leapt*. I finally found a way to still the yearning inside of me, and provide for my family at the same time. I auditioned, and landed the lead guitar spot on the second team. Weeks turned into months, and I ended up playing on both teams. Then, as attendance grew and services were added, we added a third team, and I played on it, as well. I couldn't get enough of it. I was looking forward to the next weekend as soon as we started packing up our gear on Sunday morning.

However, there was a discrepancy. While my weekends playing at church were a peaceful, happy time, my weeks spent at my job were steadily getting worse. I was being scheduled to work crazy hours, often working two midnight shifts, an afternoon shift, and two morning shifts in the same week. The lack of sleep I was suffering due to this made my home life awful, with me treating my wife and son in less-than-ideal ways due to my short temper and irritability. The job costing me proper rest was one thing, but the weekends of playing guitar actually made things worse, because it was a glimpse of what things could be like if I was making my living at music. A window into my "could have been."

Finally, one crazy morning, after I had worked 22 of the previous 30 hours, things changed, and in a hurry. One discussion with my boss turned into an argument, which turned into a shouting match, which ended with me being let go. Great. No means of providing for my family. I knew I had to get another job as soon as possible, but the thought of another 9-5 job made me feel ill. I felt lost. I wanted so badly to get back into music, but I couldn't get the courage up to look into it, or even confess that desire to my wife. I was so frightened of turning into the man my family had told me I had chosen to be...a selfish person who put his own desires over the needs of his family

While I was in the middle of agonizing over what to do next, Misty sat me down for a talk. She told me that she cared more about me being happy than how much money I made. That no matter what my family thought, she was confident that I was good enough to be able to do what I loved while supporting the family. She suggested that I put up some fliers locally offering guitar lessons and while I built my student list, she would make up the slack. She also knew that I had been dreaming about someday building guitars, and surprised me on Father's Day that year with a wood blank for a guitar body, and a book on how to build them.

Little by little, my fears grew smaller as my guitar studio grew bigger.

I taught both out of my church, and then the local music store. I started gigging regularly with a local Christian artist and also started a Top 40 cover band for doing corporate events and weddings.

With no "regular" job, I was also freed up to become even more involved in our church's music ministry. As I spent more time helping out at the church, I felt more and more like I was supposed to be there. I felt almost a tidal pull in my heart, drawing me toward music ministry. It was the oddest, yet most amazing, thing I'd ever felt. I was the most complete I had ever been. Like I was the "me-est" me I could be.

Looking back at that time of transition, I can't help but be amazed by the support given to us by countless friends who encouraged us through the tough parts, and especially by my wife Misty. Her patience, love, and support helped me to see through the fears that had plagued me about living the life I was created to live.

I had read 1 John 4:18 many times, but it took this season of my life to really understand how perfect love can, and does, cast out fear. That provision is cooler than anything else.

5

Overcoming a Fear of Failure One Step at a Time

By Janet Oberholtzer

Finally, my boys were not only in bed, but they were sleeping. It had been a normal bedtime… nothing too chaotic, but as usual it was one more story, one more glass of water, one more hug and one more good-night before they morphed from active preschoolers into sleeping angels.

As usual, I relaxed on the couch with a book ready to get lost in another world now that the house was quiet. But that night I couldn't focus on reading. My mind kept wandering back to something circling through my brain … running.

I was 28 years old, starting a business with my husband and raising three sons, ages four and under. I needed something for me. Something to maintain my sanity. Through a series of events, running became my focus. But I was scared to try it.

Running is a fairly basic process. Put one foot in front of the other at a faster pace than when you are walking. I'd been walking since I was one… so how difficult could running be?

As I tried to figure out what was holding me back, I heard the voices. Those voices. The ones that feed my fear of failure.
Lazy.
Dumb.
Stupid.
No good.
You can't do that.
You disappoint me.
What's wrong with you?

Hearing those words (and more) while growing up caused me to develop an unhealthy fear of who I am and what I can or can't do. For too long, whenever I thought about doing anything, I first had to battle the fear of failure in my head.

In the previous decade or so, I had realized that just because someone said something negative about me didn't mean it was true. But realizing that and being able to live it out were two different things.

The process of quieting the voices had been ongoing. But many times, I felt like any steps I took forward were soon followed by almost as many steps backward.

Reading about how criticism in one's childhood (and beyond) can affect you as an adult was helpful. But as I lay on the couch that evening, I sensed that I needed to move from reading about it to applying it to my life. I needed to take a literal step in overcoming the fear of failure that often ruled my life due to choices others had made.

I began going for walks to build up strength. Then I slowly transitioned from walking to running. I liked running… it made me feel alive. But those damn voices often insisted on joining me on the runs and I worried about everything… how far I could go, what I looked like and what others would think.

Living in a small town with family and friends nearby meant any car that came by could be someone I knew. So whenever I heard a car approaching, I quickly slowed down to a walk, even pretending to pick wildflowers along the road so I'd have an excuse for being out there.

We are complex and connected. As running made my body stronger, my mind and emotions also gained strength. I was able to stifle some of those annoying voices instead of listening to them. Running gave me so many benefits, that soon I didn't care what others thought about me doing it.

A decade after I started running, a severe accident almost took my legs and my life. As I recovered, all my doctors said that running was definitely a thing of my past. At first, my pain and limitations had me agreeing with them. There was no way my beat-up body would ever run again.

Some days, I relived running through my memories. Cherishing all the experiences, friends, and opportunities that had come my way through running. Other days, that was too painful, so I tried to forget about running. To forget that it had ever been a part of my world.

Again, we are complex and connected. My battered body had the visible scars, but my emotions were just as damaged. This allowed the negative voices of the past to again invade my mind. For a few years, fear of failure parties about everything had free reign in my head.

Four years post-accident, a caring doctor preformed my last

corrective surgery, and he not only gave me permission, but also gave me encouragement to try running again.

I was thrilled and I was terrified.

I knew it takes time, energy and endurance to begin running. And with the body I now had, it would take even more. But one slow painful step at a time, I returned to running.

Pre-accident, I had gravitated to the half-marathon distance (13.1 miles) and as my body recovered, I found myself doing the same. My first half-marathon was a failure… I had to walk more than I ran. The voices in my head had a huge celebration party and were thrilled to tell me they'd been right all along.

I almost quit running for a few months. But every now and then, I'd drag myself out the door. Sometimes for a walk, sometimes for a run. Doing this made me realize I wanted to run again.

To counteract my fears, I educated myself about running with an injured body. Placing walking breaks throughout my runs seemed like a wise combination for my body. So I bought a run/walk timer and set out to increase my strength and endurance again.

I adjusted my eating habits, trained well and did another half-marathon. I felt great throughout the run and finished strong… leaving some of those negative voices on the road.

I did three more half-marathons in the next ten months. I felt good during and after the races and before I knew it I was entertaining thoughts about doing a full marathon.

Though I told others, and myself, that I was going to do one, for weeks I could not bring myself to sign up for it. A fear of failure overshadowed my desire and made me doubt my ability to do 26.2 miles. I felt like a toddler tackling a climb up Mount Everest.

For weeks I attempted to cover up my procrastination with excuses about my body, the race, the timing, the whatever! Anything to avoid making a commitment to do it. I researched and asked questions, my fears grasping for any legitimate excuse.

With my boys in their teens and beyond, evenings are much louder in our house and bedtime much later, but relaxing with a book is still part of my routine. So it's another night, another book… but again I can't focus on reading. My brain is whirling with the realization that this fear of failure isn't coming from my past anymore. I remember an inspirational saying that had circulated via email in the pre-Facebook days, complete with beautiful horses galloping across a prairie.

The past might be a good signpost, but it's a lousy hitching post.

My fear of failure might stem from the past, but now it's my own voice feeding me negative thoughts. And just like years earlier, I know to overcome this fear of failure I need to take a literal step… actually closer to 50,000 steps.

I take the first step and sign up for the full marathon. Making the commitment quiets some of my fears. Again I realize how actions are needed to defeat fears. All the correct, proper, intelligent thoughts alone can't do it.

I begin my training knowing that hard work will be key to defeating the rest of my fears and to do the marathon. The general rule of thumb is that you should work up to a 20-mile training run, because 'they' say, "if you can do 20, you can do 26.2."

With that in mind, I do 12, 14 and 16 mile training runs. Each run is hard and I can't even allow myself to think about doing 26.2 miles still looks like Mount Everest.

Despite my doubts, I do feel my body strengthen and my fear of failure lessens slightly with each run. Yet 20 miles looms ahead of me. It concerns me. I wrestle the familiar fear of failure, because it wants me to give up before I even attempt it.

The 20-mile day arrives. I begin the run still doubting that I will finish it. I keep waiting for something to go wrong. But one step at a time, running for three minutes and walking for one minute, I move through the miles.

And I do it! I do 20 freakin' miles. Yes, I'm tired, but I do it.

As I soak in a hot bath, I still cannot quite believe that what I have feared for the previous months, I have just accomplished. Yes, I still have 26.2 miles to do in a few weeks and I still have some fears about that, but for the first time Mount Everest doesn't look as threatening.

I wrinkle like a prune as I sit and ponder the lesson that I'm learning (again). If I wait until all my fears are addressed, resolved or gone before I attempt anything in life … I won't accomplish much. It's only by putting actions to my thoughts and words that I will move forward in overcoming my fear of failure.

Though fears are and always will be part of the human experience… one step at a time, I have learned that I didn't need to allow fears to stop me from attempting things I want to accomplish in life.

6

Not Afraid to be Me

By Kerry Whalen

A few years ago, at the tender age of forty-three, I completed my teaching degree. Most of the work was done at home, as a part-time, external student. Prior to the degree, I'd had a number of years' experience both teaching, and designing curriculum, in a small, alternative school. I'd also worked as a teacher's aide in a public school during my years of study. Both experiences had revealed a creative passion for teaching. I loved it, and my aptitude had been clearly recognised by those I worked with. Gaining a proper qualification seemed the obvious course. I'd done really well in all my units. I *should* have been approaching the end of my degree with confidence, and a sense of purpose and achievement.

However, it was not so. For almost seven years of study, I had been pushing down a nameless fear that would not go away. Instead of looking forward to finalising the formalities, and moving on with my obvious vocation, I was terrified. The unnamed fear worsened as I approached my final practicum. I was to spend a month teaching a year 6 class in a nearby Christian School. It was a well-established, private school with a fine reputation, there were unlikely to be serious discipline problems. I knew my stuff. It should have been smooth sailing.

The final practicum began, but I was floundering from the beginning. There were a few strong characters in the class, and no matter how much I reminded myself that they were "just twelve-year-olds" I found them intimidating. Although one of my great strengths as a teacher had always been my ability to connect well with my students, I struggled to gain any real rapport with the class. Before the prac was even half over, it was clear that I was not coping. To make matters worse, I was not even sure why. One morning, I arrived at school and could not enter the classroom. I ended up weeping in the photocopy room, unable to pull myself together, and completely unable to explain myself. My nonplussed supervisor sent me home, where I continued to weep uncontrollably. The next day was no better, or the day after that. The practicum had to be cancelled, and I continued to struggle through each day, an emotional mess.

I'd been on some hormone medication, and there was some thought that my emotional state was at least partly an adverse reaction to this. It probably *was* a factor, however a medication change did not bring about any real sense of wellness. I prayed – but it was mostly wordless weeping! I sought counselling. A few things came to light, but no great breakthroughs, and no sense of freedom or release.

As far as I could articulate, the fear I'd been choking down was fear of exactly what was happening! Fear that I would be exposed as a weak and worthless mess. After all, that's what I had always known I was. The reasons why? Well, that was harder to work out. I had struggled with depression, and with feelings of not coping, since my teen years. Even when things were going well on the surface, and I seemed to be succeeding – I always knew that another low was just around the corner. I knew that I would end up being seen for what I really was. Part of my anxiety over this particular prac, was that the children were older. Unlike the little ones, they could "see" me. I'd even mentioned my trepidation towards teaching older grades to a previous practicum supervisor. "Just remember, they are children, you are the adult." She'd said. But it seemed this was a fear that ran deep. "Just remembering" hadn't helped.

Talking things over with my mother shed some new light on my own experiences as a primary school student. I remembered being very much "on the outer", and struggling to fit in. My recollections are not very detailed but my strongest impression, when I think back, is simply an overwhelming feeling of worthlessness. I felt that being "a Miller" was somehow a repulsive thing. I've never asked any of my siblings, but I don't think they ever felt that way. I'm not sure why I did. One factor, according to mum, may have simply been the cohort of students I was part of. Apparently, it was a particularly "difficult" group. She related to me how, year after year, teachers had commented on the struggles they had with that particular mix of personalities. How there were more problems with bullying, and just a whole lot more relational difficulties than with most years. My school years had certainly not been happy, which was one of the reasons it had taken me so long to come to teaching. I recall teaching being suggested as a possible future by senior school peers, because I was "good at explaining things" – and my recoil, then, at the thought of *ever* coming back to school for anything!

My unhappy school years had been followed by a bit of a tumultuous life, marred by continuing bouts of depression, bad decisions, and some negative consequences. On the surface, things had been better for some time. I looked "settled". I was married with children, paying off a home, and doing well at my chosen career, even if it had been chosen a little late. However there were serious 'cracks' in my settled normalcy, and big chunks of my history that I didn't like to talk about. Did it all start back at school? Or was I just fundamentally flawed?

Whatever the reasons, here I was; supposedly old enough to be well and truly past all that, but completely unable to fight the same fear I'd experienced way back in primary school – fear of … ridicule? Fear of "exposure"? Fear of being "seen" as the worthless, unworthy girl I felt I was on the inside.

I finished the semester (apart from the aborted practicum). I got through my exams. Semester break gave me the opportunity to rest a little, and I was functioning more normally, although I still was not free of a continued sense of dread concerning my future, and especially the still-unfinished practicum.

Unless I was going to simply abandon the last six years of study, there was no option but to re-do the dreaded prac. Even if I never taught again, I had to get through it, to complete the degree I had worked at for so long. The prac was re-scheduled for fourth term. Same class. Same supervising teacher.

Sometime in the lead-up to Practicum: Mark II, God had shown me something. I can't remember exactly when it was, or even all the details, but it came in the form of some half-remembered words of Scripture, and affected me profoundly. Those words were "You are the righteousness of God in Christ Jesus". I'm not even sure where in the Bible they are – but it was as if God spoke them to me, personally. Even as I was questioning my own inner identity, my ability to cope, my worth as a human being – it was as if His Spirit had held up an eternal, decisive hand and said, "STOP". In a way I can't clearly explain, He spoke to my heart, telling me that it didn't matter what weaknesses and fears I had harboured on the inside. It didn't matter where I'd been, or what I'd done. He had given me HIS identity. If I belonged to Him, that meant I was beautiful, radiant, and whole – not because of anything intrinsically mine, but because He had declared it so. As I write this, it sounds kind of cheesy, like a hundred "motivational" type sermons I've heard over the years. Yet it was a deeply profound experience. It was God's heart speaking to mine, and it gave me something I could hold onto in the middle of my storm of fear.

The first day of my rescheduled prac arrived, and I found myself once again driving to school, with lesson plans on the seat beside me, and a huge knot of fear in my stomach. As my car wound slowly through morning traffic, my hands gripped the wheel, and I could feel panic rising and tears beginning to take hold. This was bad. I was feeling exactly as I had, the day my last prac had so abruptly ended. I prayed desperately, but the overwhelming panic did not subside. I drove the twenty-minute route to the school, gripping the wheel, fighting back tears, and saying out loud "I am the righteousness of God in Christ Jesus". I must have looked like some kind of nut-case, white-faced and talking to myself! But He had told me my identity was not any of those things I was afraid of. I had nothing to hold on to, except that tiny thread of hope He had given me, and I battled the fear with those words. I pushed against the panic, and the insistent dread of exposure with the tenuously held knowledge that He had given me an identity that was both powerful and beautiful.

As I pulled into the school carpark, I was almost choking with panic. I gathered my teaching materials, and a staff member greeted me from the other end of the parking lot. I smiled weakly and looked away, afraid that words would bring a flood of tears I couldn't stop. I walked towards the classroom, desperately holding on to the words God had given me. "I am the righteousness of God in Christ Jesus… I am the righteousness of God in Christ Jesus…" If I could just gain control of the panic and threatening tears… It wasn't getting better. God… Where are you??? As I walked to the classroom a wave of panic threatened to drown me, and I think the last few steps towards that door were about the hardest I've ever taken in my life. Then, as I entered the classroom, the fear left me. I could breathe. The threatening tears had not erupted, and I began to feel calm.

I was the first to arrive in the room, which was good. I took a few minutes to organise myself, feeling calmer and more in control by the minute. The day passed smoothly. I was able to successfully finish the practicum. It wasn't perfect – there were great lessons, mediocre lessons, and a few duds. There were days when I had a good rapport with the kids, and things were positive and fun, and days when I found some of them hard to handle. However, even though some days were hard, the feeling of terror never returned.

There's a bit of an "addendum" to this story. At the end of the semester, with the practicum finally completed, while I was studying for final exams, I felt drawn to stop what I was doing, just for a little, and touch base with God. I hadn't been praying a great deal (I don't, always), and things had been hectic and busy anyway. The pull on my heart was insistent – I'm sure it was God calling me to talk with Him. So I stopped, there at the dining room table amongst my books, and began to have a heart-to-heart with God. I told Him that I still felt apprehensive about a teaching career, but I believed He knew exactly what I needed, just to help build my confidence and get me where I needed to be. That was about it. Not a long conversation – but I really felt that He was present, and heard me, and I had a sense of peace. It was in His hands.

About forty minutes later, the telephone rang. It was one of the executive teachers from a school where I'd done an earlier practicum. Would I be interested in teaching there, next year? The class was a year 5/6 class. I had no hesitation in accepting. I knew it would hold challenges, but I also knew this was the right position, and I could do it.

As it turned out, the class, which I shared with another beautiful teacher, Kate, was one of *those* challenging cohorts of students that come along only rarely. Much like my own primary school cohort had been, all those years ago. In many ways, the year was a struggle. If I had not had the balancing perspective of Kate, who had been teaching in the regular system for quite some time, I would have blamed myself for the difficulties. However it was clear that it was not an easy group. There were weeks where both of us felt discouraged, and plenty of days where I know I handled the group less than wonderfully. However there were bright spots too, and through all the stress and messiness of that first year, those feelings of panic and worthlessness never returned.

I remained at that school the following year, teaching many of the same students once again. Having "found my rhythm" somewhat, and learned from a lot of my first year mistakes, I enjoyed them, this time around. The rapport that I always thought should be a part of good teaching was there, and it was a rewarding year.

We moved from that area after that, so I took a break from teaching for a little over a year (mostly to concentrate on moving and renovations, and to be there for my own children as they adjusted to a new area and new school). When I returned to teaching after the break as a casual in an unfamiliar school, I wondered if the old fear would be an issue. It wasn't. In fact, the first class I took was a year 6 class, containing quite a few feisty boys – not unlike the group I'd taken in my infamous final prac. I didn't find myself nervous at all! In fact, we had a great day together. During lunch break, when one of the other teachers commented to me that they were a "hard group", all I could do was grin!

I'm still teaching, and still enjoying it. The fear that almost stopped me from graduating (and probably from living life fully in any sense at all) was not directly teaching related, but I believe stemmed from a deep sense of personal inadequacy. Teaching, and indeed, life, does not always go smoothly. However the source of my fear was not situation-dependent. It was something at the core of my identity as a person. The healing I received was something that spoke to that identity, and named me as a valued child of God. I have not always proved myself adequate to every situation, but my identity is secure, and that crippling fear has never returned.

7

Little Blue Pills

By Richard DiPippo

"Could you come with me? We need to talk."

Those who have worked office jobs know that when your boss says this to you, nothing good ever follows.

We walked into a conference room. No one else was there. There was a box of Kleenex and a glass of water on the table.

I don't remember much of what he said. He left, and a human resources representative called me on the phone to discuss my severance pay. And then I left, never to return. I was familiar with the protocol. This was the fourth time it had happened. I felt a strange sense of relief. I had known this was coming. The company had just been bought, and I had received two consecutive poor performance reviews.

I had been at that job almost four years - a personal best for me at the time. My previous attempts had lasted six months, three months, and two weeks (that one was a working interview that didn't work out).

How had I gotten to this point? I was twenty five and had gone through three jobs in five years, yet no one had ever disputed my aptitude. I wasn't lazy, although you wouldn't know it by the prodigious amount of time I spent surfing the web while at work. I enjoyed the work I was doing, but any joy I got from work was eclipsed by anxiety and fear.

I'm a software engineer. At the time I was a junior software engineer, so my job consisted mostly of fixing software bugs rather than designing new software. Every time a new bug got assigned to me, I was seized with anxiety, wondering if it would be the one that I would be unable to fix. Never mind the fact that I figured out every one of them, eventually.

It wasn't like I was working on guidance systems for nuclear missiles, either. If I screwed up, nobody died. So what was making me panic?

Why, a serotonin imbalance, you silly goose. But I didn't know that. I was convinced that getting counseling or medication would make me a failure as a Christian. If I just prayed hard enough, read the Bible enough, and listened to enough Christian music, surely the anxiety would go away, right?

I won't say praying didn't help at all. There was an abandoned stretch of highway near my workplace, so I would go for frequent prayer walks. This made me feel better - temporarily. But whether it was an hour later or a day later, I would be back at the same point. And now, here I was, back at the same point, getting laid off again.

I got a new job pretty quickly doing the same kind of work. Soon after, my wife and I found out we were going to be my parents. My mother had always been very anxious, and my world as a child was very small as a result. She had never gotten counseling or medication, so she self-medicated by creating a strict routine and avoiding anything that made her anxious. I didn't want this for my children.

There's a courtroom scene in the movie *A Few Good Men* in which a soldier is being asked about an unofficial form of military discipline called a "Code Red". The soldier is presented with the military code of justice in book form and asked to point out the page in which a Code Red is defined. When he can't, the prosecutor smugly offers this as proof that Code Reds don't exist.

On his way back to his desk, the defense attorney snatches the book out of his hands, presents it to the witness, and asks him to point out the page that tells where the mess hall is. When he can't, the defense attorney says, with mock surprise, "Well then, how did you know where to eat?"

In much the same way, I finally decided that even though the Bible didn't mention counselors or anti-depressants, it didn't mention antibiotics or indoor plumbing either. Yet for some reason I had never had consulted it on the moral correctness of these modern conveniences.

I started seeing a counselor, and saw benefits right away. My self-confidence was higher and my anxiety was lower. Then my counselor suggested that I see a psychiatrist to see if medication could help me. I did so, and lo and behold, I walked out of the appointment with a prescription for Prozac in my hand.

I didn't fill it right away. I still wasn't sure how I felt about taking it. Shouldn't I be able to fix this problem with God's help, without medication? Then, a few months later, I got hooked on Percocet and my perspective changed.

I started taking Percocet after I had back surgery to remove a ruptured disc in my back. I became hooked in the sense that everyone who takes strong painkillers becomes hooked - I was staying within the prescribed dosage, but unbeknownst to me, my brain had quietly developed a dependency. I was concerned about staying on it too long, so when I started to feel better I drastically cut my dosage.

I was already feeling a little depressed. It was my first surgery, and a reminder that I was getting older. I hadn't fully recovered yet, and I wasn't sure what my pain level was going to be like once I did. It was a scary time. Not the time to be going cold turkey.

One night soon after cutting the dosage, I got severely depressed, to the point that I was having dark thoughts about suicide. It was as though there was a thick fog in my brain, choking out reality. Within an hour, It seemed perfectly logical that life was no longer worth living, and that I should just swallow the entire bottle of Percocet. I'd be doing my family a favor.

Somehow I worked up the nerve to tell my wife. She took my announcement in stride, looked me square in the eye, and told me to take a Percocet. I protested. She narrowed her eyes and repeated her demand. I took the pill, and ten minutes later, I was back to normal. It was like a thunderstorm had stopped, leaving only wet pavement as evidence of its existence. Whatever reservations I had about taking Prozac were gone. I filled the prescription and started taking it.

I've been taking it for about a year. Now that my brain doesn't spend so much time fighting anxiety, it has lots of free time to analyze all the other negative patterns in my life, which I'm in the process of discussing with my counselor. It's also been an interesting experience finding out what a normal level of anxiety feels like. I didn't even recognize it the first few times I felt it. When you've walked around for years with an enormous load on your back, you feel great when it's removed, but you have to adjust to walking without it.

I think my resistance to counseling and medication had more to do with pride and fear than anything spiritual. Pride that wouldn't let me admit that I needed help. Fear that the little blue pills would change me into someone else. But the anxiety was the thing that had changed me. If anything I feel more like myself now. The medicine has defanged the beast. What was once a roaring lion prowling around in my brain, devouring joy and ambition, is now a mewling kitten, easily pushed aside and dismissed.

The best part? I'm still at the new job, six years later.

8

The Last Word

By Diana R.G. Trautwein

It was a Thursday morning early in December, 1996. My dark blue Ford Escort wagon was stuffed to the roofline with this, that, and the other thing, and I was ready to begin my first 100 mile drive north to Santa Barbara from our home in the foothills of Pasadena CA. My husband came downstairs to see me off, giving me a bear hug and surprising me by bursting into tears. I could not remember the last time I'd seen him cry. "What brings these tears?" I asked. "I'm crying for you," he said. "You've never gone off to a new job like this before, you've never had to carry the load of performing for pay, you've never had to deal with the messy stuff that comes with being an employee. I have, and I know what's ahead for you."

To say I was stunned would be putting it mildly. I was leaving for a new job, a part-time associate pastorate a long ways from home, working with a lead pastor I knew moderately well and a group of people I knew not at all. I would be living in a parishioner's guesthouse four days each week while I looked for a home for us to purchase. And my sweet husband's tears sent me off on that first of many weekly jaunts in a wave of love and anxiety and a whole lot of uncertainty.

Maybe I was stepping into something I wasn't ready to do.

Why had I thought this job description fit me so perfectly? What in the world could a housewife from Pasadena have to offer a congregation in Santa Barbara? Why had I ever left the safety of home and hearth to enter seminary? Why had I left the safety of seminary to begin ministry life? Why had I not been content with the life my mother had lived – tending husband, kids, house, garden? Within a matter of hours, on the first day of my brand new job, this litany of questions brought me to the point of paralyzing terror.

What was I doing here?

That state of panic lasted right into the New Year. I was on the steep end of the learning curve, meeting new people, discovering how things worked in this place. And it seemed that every single thing I learned added yet another layer of fear to the boiling questions inside my spirit. On the outside, I was the new kid on the block, learning the ropes. On the inside, I was a mess. And as I prepared... "as I prepared to attend our annual denominational Midwinter Conference, I realized how much I needed some word from the Lord to help me deal with this lump of terror in my chest. As I searched the program schedule during my flight to Chicago, I noticed that there would be a small, daily service of communion and prayer, a welcome respite in the midst of so many large gatherings of 1400 pastors. I made a mental note to slip in and sit in the back row, so that I could worship in a space where I would not be known and where I was not in charge.

I did exactly that on my first full day at the conference. It was a small group – maybe 30 people. Just a lectern, a small table for communion, and a piano. Not a fancy, high-tech time, to say the least! But such a powerful preached word – from a man whose life and ministry I greatly appreciated. And then, the opportunity was given for anointing and blessing, and I found myself striding over to stand in the line, my heart in my throat.

After listening to my anguished admission of paralyzing fear, the presiding pastor used cool, strong hands to touch my forehead with oil and with loving care. And I heard a wise voice offering these words: "Lord of Love, give Diana the gift of *your* love for the people to whom you have called her, for we know that *only love can cast out fear.*" Just that, nothing more. Straight, simple words, spoken directly from the heart of God, through this kind, humble man, to a frightened child.

And then, like a mantle from on high, I actually felt that gift of love descend upon me, shoving aside the terror and filling me with something holy, something whole. It was entirely grace – a gift, a blessing, an anointing. For the next 14 years, I carried that mantle with me every single day of my ministry. Yes, I was anxious and uncertain again - lots of times! But the grip of terror had been loosened, permanently.

When I accepted the call of God - first to seminary, then to pastoral ministry, then to unpaid work in my home church while I finished the hoop-jumping for ordination, and finally, to a paid position for the first time in my life at the age of 52, I had no clue what was coming. None. And those initial days and weeks in Santa Barbara were lived with trembling hands and heart, and the sinking sensation that I was just *not up to this.*

Fear is corrosive, invasive and real and it can sometimes really mess with the work of God within us. What came to me as I stood and received that oil on my head and those words in my heart was this:

God is greater than our fear. Love is greater than our fear. And if we ask for love - or if we invite someone else to ask on our behalf - God will give it. Yes, God will give it.

What came with that job, that call, those dear people whom I was able to love with a Love way beyond my own capacity, was a whole lot of pain and struggle; and a whole lot of indescribably wonderful joy. Together we weathered the loss of a senior pastor of 23 years - gone to Chicago for a denominational position. Immediately followed by the loss of a staff pastor for moral reasons. And, of course, there was the groundbreaking and construction of a worship center and gathered-together-in-one-hallway office space, the culmination of a careful, prayerful 10-year plan, all of it happening *during this time without a permanent senior pastor.* Thankfully, we had a great Interim Pastor whose gifts were a great complement to my own and, by the grace of God, we survived those two years.

And there was more: four months after construction ended, we called a new lead pastor. Over the next few years, while he was out of town for either professional or personal reasons, the congregation and I weathered both the suicide of a much-loved elder, and about six months later, a raging wildfire that destroyed the homes of 14 families in our congregation and seriously damaged six others.

If I had had the slightest glimmer about any of this during those initial weeks of terror, I would have scurried back to housewifery in a heartbeat. But I didn't know. I couldn't know. God, however, did. Working through a sensitive servant-leader in a small communion service, God gave me both a message and a gift: **love is the answer**.

Not trite, sugary, greeting-card kind of 'love,' but nitty-gritty, stand-in-the-trenches-together kind of love. Going to the hospital and singing while a loved friend passes to the next life kind of love. Counseling couples and individuals through difficult life situations kind of love. Riding the sometimes difficult currents of church politics kind of love. Baptizing babies and adults, offering the bread and the cup, preaching the Word, teaching, organizing retreats and seminars, hosting meetings and small groups and committees kind of love. Crying with those whose children or partners are struggling with addictions kind of love. Planning creative ways to include liturgy and silence in worship kind of love. Teaching middle-school students about the wonders of grace in confirmation classes kind of love. Writing annual reports and birthday cards and sympathy cards and thank you notes kind of love.

None of it was easy - all of it was *good.*

And not one second of it was my own doing. Without the gift of love - the kind of love that the apostle John writes about in his first letter, the kind that casts out fear - my journey would have been a very different one. In fact, I doubt that I would have lasted more than about a year. Whenever I was tempted to throw in the towel, from exhaustion or frustration or pique, it was love that came to the rescue. Always, always - no matter what else I was feeling and thinking - the wonderful weight of that mantle reminded me that there was still good work to be done, good people to be pastored. This is the story I told at my retirement dinner at the end of 2010 - the story that began with my husband's sweet tears, continued with that gift received in a Chicago hotel basement, and played itself out in good times and bad over my tenure at that church." . And this is the story I still tell today: **fear does not have the last word - love does.** Thanks be to God.

9

Of Fear and Faithfulness

By Addie Zierman

The thing about the rejection – about the *fear of rejection* – is that it doesn't ever get easier.

You write. You send. You write. You send.

You spend hours crafting a paragraph, following a thought. You're erasing and rewriting and reimaging and it's hard, draining work. You pour your stories onto the page like perfume, and they are all that you own, all that you really have in the world.

You pour them out until they are gone, and then you send it.

***

I came across the *creative nonfiction* genre in college, a little bit by accident. It felt like finding that thing you didn't know that you absolutely needed on a garage sale table for a quarter. You grab it, pay for it, and spend the rest of the day feeling victorious and lucky. You wonder how others walked by it, didn't notice that *This Is The Perfect Thing!* You wonder why anyone would give it away *for a quarter.*

It's sometimes called *memoir*, sometimes *narrative* or *essay*, but in the end, it's the truth of your life made into art. It's small little stories that tap into a much bigger stories, a way to connect the pieces of your past and then connect your past to your present. To other people's present.

I loved it immediately. I wrote into it with abandon.

And then I discovered exactly why it was on the 25-cent table in the first place: it's because of what it demands. Truth. Transparency.

When you choose to work with the shattered pieces of your own true life, your fingers get a little bloody. When you choose to present yourself as you truly are – no makeup, hair gnarled, dark circles under your eyes – you have to let go, a little, of what you wish you were, what you believe yourself to be.

When you write creative nonfiction or memoir or essay, there are no characters to deflect the attention, no plot twists to throw readers off the trail. It's just you. They know it's you. And *you* know it's you.

It doesn't stop me from loving the whole weird genre, but it makes it a little heavier. A little harder to hold.

I write and send and write and send, and writing and real life get all tangled together. An editor or a professor or reader might pull at a careless word or phrase, and it tugs that tender place in my heart where the truth came from, where it still lives.

***

The letters come and they keep coming. Whether they come in the afternoon mail or appear instantly in my inbox, they have the same grainy language. Vague and impersonal. Apologetic but distant.

"We've decided to pass," they say.

"We get a large number of excellent submissions," they remind.

"Please consider us again in the future," they suggest.

Sometimes it's just silence. Days of it that build into months that build into a heavy, closed door.

This is the language of rejection, and my heart feels dense and weighty at the sound of it. The polite *No thank you* is as harsh and unexpected as a punch to the gut, and I end up with a bruise that I can't see but that I feel for days.

When I tell you that I'm afraid of *rejection*, it's not so much these words in all of these emails. It's not even the silence. The rejection itself is just the container. It's the white sheet over the ghost: the fabric itself is not so scary. That vague, invisible thing beneath it that moves of its own accord – that is terrifying.

The thing under the thing pulses with all of the words I struggle not to believe about myself. You are not good enough. You are not important. Your words are worthless, your stories are small. You're not funny enough. Not brilliant enough. Not loveable or likeable or wanted.

It carries the heavy emptiness of abandonment. *Reject:* To refuse to accept, consider, submit to, hear, take, or use. To spew out, like you would something sour. To cast aside, discard, drop. To sweep away like a cobweb. It's like a body does with an incompatible organ, the whole of the immune system turning in on that with is foreign to it. *Rejecting.*

During my clearer moments, it's possible to talk some sense into myself. I sit at the kitchen counter, the rejection up on the computer screen. I am stern with myself as I speak the truth. *This is not about you,* I say. *It's not* personal. *It's business.*

But at night, when I'm in bed, and the house is quiet and the dog is shifting around by my feet, I can see that ghost hovering so clearly above me, and I am paralyzed with fear and inadequacy.

What if I write it all out and no one wants it? What if I give my whole self to the world, and they turn around and give it right back?

In the dark of night, I am acutely aware of how much I want to matter. Of how afraid I am of not mattering at all.

***

The woman who taught me about creative nonfiction also taught me about God.

She was a professor at my small, evangelical college, but she spoke of Jesus in a way that was decidedly un-evangelical. She was about stillness. About listening. About the way that art and faith are inextricably linked.

She lit into my early drafts mercilessly, her green pen crossing out entire pages of hard-won words. She wrote *Push* in the sections where I thought I'd gone as far as I could go. She wrote *Not sure…* in the sections where I thought I was sure.

The evangelical culture was in growth-mode, coming up with measurable goals to assess the success of its various programs. But she stood in front of us, calm, still. She moved slowly and purposefully, taking time to gather books and to walk to the next place.

She kept a file full of her rejection letters rather than throwing them away. She said, "There is no success, no failure. There is only faithfulness and faithlessness."

No success. No failure. In the end, there is just a calling.

The call is pressed upon our lives and it beacons, and we respond either by giving ourselves to it or by tuning it out. Faithfulness. Faithlessness.

After all, who among us can say what God will do with these words that we spill like perfume on the page? Who can know what he will do with the stories that we give to him freely, the truth laid bare on the page because we believe that, in the end, it will set us free?

I am afraid. I am terrified. I send my words into the void, and my heart beats abnormally for the next couple of days.

The rejections come. It is a kind of labor to write them into my spreadsheet, to create a record of this work, and to know that still, it's worth it. This is the flesh-and-blood reality of faithfulness: the feel of the computer keys under my fingers; the way that *Rejected* looks typed red on the screen.

But this is my work. My calling. I picked it up off the clearance garage-sale table all those years ago, and it fit perfectly in the palm of my hand. I knew it then; I know it still today.

I hold this tension: I am afraid. I am faithful.

I write another story, essay, chapter. I cast it along with my heart into the wild wind.

I count it as gain even when it feels like loss.

10

Surviving a Speech with Nail Polish and a Notebook

By Tamara Lunardo

It was two days before I was to fly to Nashville for my first speaking opportunity and I was what you might call *freaking the hell out*. I was mostly excited and a little nervous to be making my first-ever solo trek through an airport, a flight, and a new city without blindly following a directionally unimpaired person. But more than that, I was a little excited and mostly nervous to be giving my first talk to a group of adults who would surely take notice if I lost all coherent verbal ability mid-message.

It should have been no sweat. I had performed in dance recitals since I could walk; I did theater all my life; I was on the speech and debate team (1997 Duo Interpretation State Champions, *if you must know*); I was a vocal performance major; I taught children music and Sunday School; I was a worship leader. But it wasn't no sweat; it was lots of sweat and swears and tears. Because I would be doing something I wanted badly to do, and I was terrified that I would do badly. I would not have a script or rehearsals; I would not be able to call "line!" It would just be me and my thoughts without the safety of a keyboard, and I thought the damn Killer Tribes Conference might just in fact kill me.

I remembered that not so long ago I had spoken shaky, impromptu words to the people of my church about setting aside our comfort to become a comfort to others, and I dashed off an email to the friend who has an MP3 of those words that were now coming back to bite me in the smarty-pants:

I WAS A FUCKING IDIOT.

Please destroy all copies of that audio. Thankyouverymuch.

***

Day before departure, and I had packed two-thirds of my wardrobe for a two-day trip because I like to be prepared, and it's easier to achieve this by overestimating your need for sweaters, tank tops, and varied footwear than it is by attempting to write a speech outline upon which you have placed egregious importance.

I struggled to structure all my thoughts and anecdotes, the important ideas and the just-so wording, rearranging them on my computer screen with the frustrating futility of assembling a picture with pieces from three different puzzles. That night was no more productive than any of its recent predecessors, but I fought against it as long as I could, desperate to fashion a life-preserver for the most-assuredly-Killer Tribes Conference.

In the end, it was nail polish that defeated me that night. I had envisioned wearing the gunmetal color on my fingers because it is a little artsy and a little edgy and a lot *me*, and the gawddamn stuff was missing. It was not where it was supposed to be or in any other evident location despite my frantic 2am search, and I had planned on it, and I needed it, and of course I could not use another color, especially not the one already on my toes as my husband suggested because THAT WOULD BE MATCHY-MATCHY, and there was just no way I could get on that plane the next morning. Fuck.

***

I sat on the aisle seat beside a pair of middle-aged Midwestern ladies, at ease with my company because there is something comforting about a culture that so highly values casseroles. We landed in Music City, and I didn't know it then, but I'd be so busy that I'd never hear any music; still, walking through an unfamiliar airport and out into the air of a new city confidently alone, I felt in some way I'd arrived.

I met a friend for lunch at the sort of hipster joint where you tolerate their condescension toward your innocent request for a Diet Coke because their portabella asiago crêpes are so good they can get away with it. We talked easily and laughed heartily, and I left with more gifts from him than he might have realized because sometimes just the right words at just the right time are exactly enough.

My gracious weekend hostess and I visited her favorite place for fruit tea, and I sat with the black fabric notebook my son had given me for Christmas because he knows I need to get out words to be the best and truest me, and I finally and simply got them out.

***

We had spent the night before in a clamorous coffee shop, moving beyond Twitter names and blog comments into real-life hugs and riotous laughter, and now we would spend the day in side-by-side seats, groups of friends long established, now expanding and enriching. They all took notes and sent Tweets except me, partly because my phone had decided to strap a chastity belt around its security access and mostly because I was too busy with intense self-preoccupation.

My talk wasn't until after lunch, so I spent the morning sessions demanding my brain learn something from the conference while my brain obstinately opted to measure my novice potential against every professional speaker's performance.

I ate just enough not to pass out and left the bounty of the greenroom for the solitude of the empty Sunday school room with my name on a sign just outside it. Rows of chairs were lined up, expectantly facing a slender white stool upon which sat a blue gift bag and a note. The presents inside were a bag of deeply aromatic coffee and a sleek mug inscribed "Killer Tribes," but the note bore witness of the real gift.

I had taken a risk to get the gig in the first place, and the risk in actually showing up for it was bigger. But the conference host had written the note presupposing my victory. He didn't say he thought I would kick ass; he declared that I already had.

The people filled my room, looked up, and waited for a moment, and it was just very *me* on my perch with the found gunmetal polish on my nails and the filled black notebook on my lap. And sometimes just the right words at just the right time are exactly enough.

So I began.

11

Unfit

By Sonny Lemmons

A few years back, I decided to finally apply for seminary. I knew that based on my age and life experiences my application and candidacy might make me stand out a bit, having not taken the typical straight-to-seminary path following the completion of my undergraduate degree that most others did. However, I felt that based on the work I had done with college students, junior and high school ministries, and serving on the creative and teaching teams for the past few years at the church I was attending was pretty much God's not-quite-subtle way of telling me that it was finally time to go down the "full time and get paid for it" ministerial path He had set my heart on half a lifetime ago.

Collecting and prepping all of my academic work was easy. The essay I needed to write? Piece of cake. But when I came to the rather personal portion of the application - labeled under "Character Questionnaire" - my heart stopped cold at what they were asking me to write about: had I ever used illegal drugs? If so, was I currently still using them? What sexual sins did I struggle with? Did I drink alcohol? If so, was I willing to sign a covenant that I would stop? Was I divorced or separated? I noticed that there was a small asterisk after one of these questions, so I followed the page down to see what it said. When I read the words printed there, my heart broke.

"While divorce does not automatically disqualify applicants from admission, please bear in mind that individuals who are divorced may be limited in their vocational options within the church, as individuals who are divorced are Biblically unfit for many leadership opportunities, including pastoral roles."

Unfit.

Because of my past.

After dealing with the emotional hell of losing what I believed and trusted was going to be my future. After falling further away from God through anger, outright rebellion, and soul-wracking despair than I ever thought possible. After days, weeks, months, years of abusing my mental and physical health through sleep and food deprivation.

After living in terror that no one would ever see anything of any worth in me ever again.

After years of therapy, innumerable tears, and the struggle to rediscover my identity. After beginning to regain a sense of self worth. After rediscovering the faith to hold on to a promise of forgiveness and being made whole and clean again. After finally allowing myself to feel worthy of being loved. After receiving the grace offered to me from God and learning to forgive myself.

I was considered unfit. To be in ministry.

By their standards.

A man who was demon possessed.

A woman who was caught in adultery.

A friend who denied Him and cursed His name in public.

A murderer.

We read in the Bible about each of these people being able to carry the message of the gospel despite their histories. Today, we hold them up as examples of how God can redeem and reclaim even the most shattered of lives. When their sins were forgiven, as promised, they were also forgotten by God. And though some may have questioned if this was indeed the same person speaking that they may have known, the power of their changed lives overshadowed the "dirtiness" of their pasts.

Pornographers.

Drug addicts.

Child molesters.

Terrorists.

Each of these labels, no matter how shocking and revolting, when preceded by the word "former" loses some of its impact and power through the forgiveness offered in the shadow of the cross. We love them. We welcome their stories. We share in the joy of their rebirth. And in the telling of their stories, they minister. To the fellow broken. To the ones who, there but for the grace of God, go themselves.

I have repeatedly referred to myself a "mutt in ministry" because I do not carry the "pedigree" of a Master of Divinity degree or any seminary training. Not that I consistently think of myself as a dog, but the comparison isn't difficult to avoid. When looking for a pet, many people feel safer in getting one from a reputable pet store because the dog in question comes with papers. They outline the training he has had. They verify he's had his shots. And yet, numerous dogs in shelters go unclaimed. Unwanted. Many have been abused, neglected or were abandoned. But like the most perfectly pedigreed of dogs, these mutts have just as much love to give.

Sometimes more, because they - we - are truly thankful for a second chance at love. And acceptance. And a family.

I'll admit though that at times, this is kind of a fun label to have. In naming myself this, I get to own my standing. Through His mercy and grace, God has allowed me to serve and continues to grant me opportunities to serve and lead in a number of capacities in the churches I have been a part of. But I am not blind to the fact that if I had just a few more letters that came after the end of my name, more people might accept me, take me seriously, or give me a chance. And I stay constantly afraid that at some point, someone will stand up and confirm my fear and insecurities that the lack of a suffix or title makes me not "legitimate" in ministry.

Compounding my concerns is that a well-intentioned person once told me I should hurry up and go to seminary sooner rather than later, because the longer I waited to get an MDiv or Ph.D., the greater the distance from when schools, churches, or organizations might find me useable. A lot of the time, individuals who jump into full-time ministry do so coming straight out of college. Because, of course, people in their early-to-mid twenties have all the answers, have their theology completely fleshed out, and are spiritually and emotionally at the apex of their maturity. Due the fact that my turn at starting in ministry didn't truly begin until after I had passed the biological age when Jesus' earthly ministry had ended, I was already behind the curve of when and how I could apparently be effective.

So I threw away my application. I gave up on this dream and calling yet again, because I was afraid. That they - the ever powerful, omnipresent "they" - were right. I was too old. I was too broken. I was indeed unfit. And because of these fears, I put up large, impenetrable walls to safeguard my heart. I started giving vague, evasive non-answers whenever someone would ask about my history, fearing that if someone knew about the reality of my past, it would forever change their opinion of me. My scarlet "D" would be glowing almost as much as the scarlet on my cheeks from embarrassment of having to admit to the less-than-perfect life and background which individuals in ministry are apparently supposed to come from. It is safe and acceptable to let the former addict speak in church, but not let them lead it.

It was not until I had a chance encounter with a person I met on Twitter that I opened up fully about my past for the first time in my life with a total stranger. And when they did not turn away or pick up stones to hurl my way, I felt something settle on me that I had never felt before: peace. That perfect peace that casts out all fear. And this peace began to morph into strength and courage to share the truth of the me of who I am. Because as I have learned, to not speak of the healing that has taken place in my life is in many ways to deny the strength and the power of the redemption I have been given. And the last thing I want to do is by my inaction is to cheapen the grace shown to me.

Dealing with the glass ceiling of my age has been comparatively easier for me, especially since I neither look nor often act anything close to my biological age. I believe that this is in some ways God making up for the years that "the swarming locust" had eaten (Joel 2:25 NASB). The years of my life that I lost to darkness are being replaced with years now and to come in serving Him. I may not be able to age backwards nor can I go back in time to stop myself from making the same mistakes, but that does not mean that this promise rings any less true. And if I can be young in my heart, then I can be youthful in attitude but still have the maturity of an individual who has gone down this life path.

Coming clean and not holding back about your past does carry a bit of anxiety with it. We all "have a friend" who has judged others or has been judged because of their past. Surviving a divorce in many ways causes you to shrink back to the heart of a child who lives in fear of not being loved. Unlike other wounds and sins, which can remain private forever, divorce is uncomfortably public. And so is the corresponding shame and pain that accompanies it.

To be candid, I am too close to the subject to be objective in the debate over the Biblical interpretation of if a divorced individual can or should work in ministry. However, when those who are in a position of power to dictate who is or is not "appropriate" to live out what they believe is a calling on their life tells you "no, you are not worthy," it is like tying yet another millstone around the neck of a soul who has struggled for years to remove the ones they themselves placed there earlier.

What God has called clean, do not call unclean.

Whom God has made clean, do not call unclean.

Or unfit.

Fear and Your Faith

Introduction

By Alise Wright

I never thought that I was in an abusive church. Even when things were really terrible, it was difficult for me to look at what was happening and think, "There is spiritual abuse happening here."

And yet when I look back on it now, there is no question that is just what was going on.

I have been a Christian for as long as I can remember. My parents took me to church from infancy and I can't think of a time in my life when I ever skipped more than a Sunday or two in a row. Missing church just felt wrong.

So when I found myself dreading going back to church for the sixth week in a row, I knew that something was amiss. This wasn't the person that I was. I was the girl who went to church without fail. I didn't walk out on church. I certainly wasn't afraid of the church.

And yet, because of that abuse, fear filled me. It came out in tears each Sunday as I would listen to the musicians play and listen to the minister preach. No matter what the sermon was about, I would hear only the voice of the accuser. Idolater. Arrogant. Unsubmissive. Quitter. Each week I would attend a church that had no connection with the abusive church, but each week, that hurtful voice was the only one I could hear.

The most awful thing about abuse is how it causes you to doubt things that you know are true. I knew what I was called to do as a Christian, but because of years of doubt being cast on that talent, I began to embrace that doubt for myself. It wormed its way deep inside of me and even though I knew that it was a lie, it bore enough resemblance to the truth that it became a perverted kind of truth in my mind.

I began to question everything that I believed about the goodness of God as a result of this abuse. I saw not a giver of good gifts, but instead as a dissatisfied being who gave gifts only to put us through some kind of twisted test to make sure that we didn't put anything above God. I looked at each day not as an opportunity to bless God with my talents, but instead as an opportunity to mess up. I didn't see God as particularly wrathful, but as constantly disappointed in me. I was supposed to be beloved, but more I believed that I was seen as a mistake; one who could never really worship the way that God intended.

This fear and depression continued for more than a year. I had been through something similar before and promised that I would never allow it to steal my joy like that had, but once again, I found myself in the midst of a deep depression that refused to lift.

This fear wasn't contained to the area of wounding, but instead touched all areas of my life. Due to the hurt that I experienced in this church, I not only stopped performing any kind of music, I also stopped writing. I stopped taking care of myself and my family. I neglected friendships.

And there was a rift between me and God. Prayer felt like a chore. I stopped reading the Bible because I feared that if I read something that felt like the voice of God, it would morph into the voice of my accusers. For so long, I felt like there could be no peace in my life.

But healing did come, bit by bit. I found a church that affirmed my talents and allowed them to flourish in ways that I had never experienced. I sought out different opportunities to play. I began to write with a conviction that I had previously been afraid to embrace.

I began to hear God again. Not in any kind of audible way, but through the interactions that I had with people who were safe and loving. Through experiences that affirmed me. As I began to listen to the voices of those who were encouraging me, and thus to the voice of God, it began to drown out the accusing, negative voices. Fear was replaced with courage. Timidity was replaced with boldness.

In the following years, changes happened that previously would have taken my already fragile faith and broken it entirely, but because of love, I was able to respond to them in a way that strengthened those relationships and also strengthened my faith. Instead of finding these experiences to be laced with angst, they were filled with peace.

I am not alone in finding fear in the midst of faith. Sadly, it is far more common than it ever should be. Sarah shares how legalism in the church caused her to have panic attacks that drove her away for years. Lore gives us a glimpse of her struggle with her perception of beauty and how it kept her from understanding fully the way that God sees her as a beautiful creation. Sonny allows us to see how his divorce affected his ability to work in church leadership and how the church can be wounding to those who most need healing.

Unfortunately, there can be deep pain inflicted by people, as you will read in the following pages. However, as we seek out those who are beacons of light in the darkness, we can overcome our fears and begin to rebuild faith. We can begin to hear God speak to us once again and we can begin to trust the words that say to us, "Peace, be still."

12

Nothing & Everything

By Melody Harrison Hanson

Some days are clues that no matter how far you've come,

you are nothing.

(And you are everything.)

Nothing and everything to the Divine and Holy One who loves, accepts, heals, guides, and knows

you.

The Holy One *loves* you no matter how often you stumble.

The Holy One *accepts* you for everything you are today and *sees* who you are becoming.

For this Creator God made you, even chose you and is the architect of your life.

The Holy One *heals,* because we sure need a healing. Especially when confronted by the hideous ogre of our envy and pride.

The Holy One *guides* and has a plan.

"Even for me?" I cry, in the shadowy, nocturnal hours of fear, anger, twisted truths, ignorance, self-delusion and distrust?

"YES, even you" whispers The Holy One.

The Holy One *knows* me better than I know myself,

leads me through the dark *sheol* of my own creating.

Patiently, kindly pulling me back when my motives, impure and self-seeking, make a collision course with life.

The Holy One is the perfect parent, *understanding* what I need, who I am and who I will become.

This Holy One *believes* when I cannot believe in myself.

For I know I am so frequently frail,

failing,

falling,

far,

from the Holy One

who *knows* all, *knows* me, *knows* the future.

Even these days

when through my streaming hot tears of shame and regret, I can only look up.

"YES, even you" whispers The Holy One.

Some days.

Some days are cues to humble you. To learn that no matter

if you are nothing, you are everything

to *the Holy One.*

13

Soaring High Above Fear

By Aletheia Schmidt

Vivid imagination. Scary dreams. Creepers in the dark; I was 5 then 6. Riding in the van. Asking dad if I had 'done it right.' Wanted to be sure I'd make it into heaven. Worried about this righteous God; I was 9. Hall light on. Worship music playing. Couldn't stop shaking while home alone. Fear of the unknown. Was I safe? I was 11. Obsessing about others, caring too much about what they thought. Sick to my stomach; I was 13. Bringing home less than perfect. Afraid that I would never be 'good enough.' Worry; I was 14. Begging God to let me marry the first guy I loved. Fear of never being loved. Fear of being alone forever; I was 15. Afraid to go to sleep. Afraid to wake up. Doubt that God wasn't who I thought God was or should be. Anxious; I was 25. Terrified that love would walk away from me. Terrified of rejection; I was 27. Petrified that my biggest fear--that love would eventually leave--would break me; I was and I am 29.

When it comes to being afraid, my life is like a speckled ceiling. Sure, there is a base coat underneath, but it's hard to notice with all the other more vibrant and fantastic colors and textures that have been painted over it: It is this top coat to which viewers are always more drawn.

Fear has been the consistent top layer throughout my life. Like a villain in a popup book, fear lurked around corners, seizing the heroine at the worst possible moment.

And beneath it all, inner doubts of wondering if I had what it took, outer confessions that I didn't, and other people's--men, friends--rejections fed the fear, and I grew from a frightened little girl to an anxious young woman. For years I struggled with the inability to move past self-doubt. In fact, in a journal entry from 1998, I wrote this:

I guess this will always be my 'lot.' I will always hate the way I look. I will always struggle with who I am and I think I will always doubt that someone would or could love me. How could I not?!

14 years later, a few months after an incredibly hard breakup, I found myself writing a different story:

When I slow myself down and ponder the past eleven months even my body knows the significance. I can't help but raise my eyebrows, tilt my head ever-so-slightly to the right, clench my jaw a bit and ask (sometimes, out loud), "Really? Did all of that happen in one year's time? Did I really date those guys, stand in those weddings, have those conversations, cry that often, and struggle that much with jealousy and discontentment?

And is it really true that somehow, in the same year, I encountered such an intense filling and fulfillment that even the parts of me that I had yet to know what they needed, found life and nourishment? That I found myself for the first time ever living from a place of not simply believing the Lord's love for me, but receiving it too? That I find myself loving, being proud of, and taking time to celebrate who I am, what I'm about, and the creativity that finds its way from my heart onto canvas and yupo paper?

What a compilation of messy, beautiful, surprising, crushing and then not-crushing 1/29th of my life. And yet, there's nothing else I would have chosen, nothing else I would have done differently. All the heartache and all the "that's so unfairs" have been worth it. And all the open doors and possibilities have been greater than I could have envisioned.

This has undoubtedly been the most transformative year of my life. And it all has to do with this: I faced my greatest fear. But more than facing my greatest fear, and more than somehow muddling my way through, I emerged stronger than I had ever thought possible, more secure and confident than I had ever imagined, and more healed and whole than I had even prayed for.

This year love looked me in the face and decided it couldn't stay: Rejection at its fullest, disappointment as its craziest, uncertainty at its loudest, and fear at its greatest.

But this year, this blessed year, I cowered no longer. No. This year I looked it square in the face and said, "Ok."

This year, this blessed year, I discovered that I was ok. That I am ok. Actually, I'm the best I've ever been. I think I'm finally beginning to understand what John means when he talks about Perfect love driving out fear (1 John 4:18). For a fearful daughter, this Father's love has been perfect (and oh my does it ever drive out the fear!).

This year, this perfect love has unlocked the cage and opened the window of my heart. This year, in this perfect love, my wings have been strengthened, extended; They are craving exercise. And this year, in this perfect love, the sun is bright and the sky is clear;

I'm ready to fly.

Actually I'm flying.

Not perfectly, or without incident, but I'm loving the view, caught-up in the adventure, chillin' in the winds, and looking for friends with whom to scour the land.

Wanna join?

14

Exiting the Panic Room

By Sarah Bost-Askins

Coal black night pressed upon my chest. The air grew hot and thick as I lay staring up at the popcorn ceiling of my dorm room. Each second, I panted for air, anything besides this oppressive mugginess entering and exiting my lungs. When I wasn't gasping for breath, I whispered one quick prayer—"Save me, Jesus." My dorm room shrank and trembled, and my body felt like a supernatural presence lifted it from the bed and dropped it down. Over and over, this sequence replayed that night. All I could do was pray three words—"Save me, Jesus."

After several eternal moments of mental agony, I stumbled out of my bed and entered dimly lit hallway nearly running into my roommate. From my facial expression, she pushed the door open and maneuvered me back to my bed. We sat quietly. Her arms around my shoulders held me tightly, and she waited till I could find the words to explain my fear. How would I explain the terror, the prayer, the escape.

"What happened?" she asked still holding my shoulders. I wanted to tell her the whole story, the dark presence, the words I choked out in prayer, but I couldn't.

"Just a nightmare," I lied. Even then, I knew this wasn't just a bad dream that one has after eating too much pepperoni pizza. It was a full-blown panic attack brought on by all the fear that I stuffed inside.

"Have you been reading this much?" she asked picking up my used copy of Harry Potter. "Maybe, you shouldn't read it. Since it's about witches and stuff." I nodded agreeing with her. I never told her that my class work and research papers devoured any free time. For several weeks, Harry Potter lay abandoned on my nightstand waiting for graduation and a few moments to read freely again.

"Yeah, guess it's not good for me," I said and stuffed the book in my desk shelf. After a few more moments of silence, we turned off the light and went back to bed. To my relief, the room returned to its normal, a peaceful refuge rather than the dark panic room it had been.

Looking back almost ten years later, I know this panic attack was fear induced. Worst of all, the fear grew out of my faith, more specifically, the church. I grew up in an independent evangelical fundamentalist Baptist church. Every Sunday, the altar call included images of fire and brimstone and isolation. This is where I learned to embrace fear. During my childhood and teenage years, I learned who to fear, what to fear, and why to fear. Gory battle metaphors against Satan and his demons peppered youth group lessons and overflowed into my pastor's sermons. Sadly, I couldn't live on a steady diet of fear-mongering before fear and my faith became inseparable. That dark night proved that fear poisoned every level of mind, body, and soul.

After first the panic attack, I lived in fear that it would happen again. Before bed, I prayed the same three words—"Save me, Jesus."

I needed to guard my mind, to prevent Satan or his hordes from entering. Those words served as my lucky rabbit's paw. But it didn't work every time. Fear bubbled and simmered during the day and poured out at night. There was no refuge, no safe haven. I turned to the church, to Bible reading, to Christian fellowship, but each one pointed out my flaws and added new things to fear. I couldn't escape the cycle. Too many nights, I spent laying awake trembling before a God who didn't release me from these chains. I thought He had given up trying to save me, but I still kept praying my lucky prayer just in case I would gain some relief.

But panic filled nights weren't the only thing I feared. The church added new things each Sunday. If the sermon wasn't about Satan and spiritual warfare, it delineated in three alliterative points how to know if I were truly "saved." A long list of commands, the rules governing my faith placed another link in my chains. Bible study should be done in the morning giving God the rightful place in my day, but I wasn't a morning person. I should relish all the door slammed in my face as we students canvased the area with tracts and invitations to church. But I couldn't. I thought we were simply pissing our neighbors off and believing their rudeness to be spiritual warfare. I should be preparing myself to be submissive, quiet wife. But I couldn't— too outspoken, too feminist. The list never ended, and neither did my fear.

If following the rules didn't induce enough panic, I feared being left behind after the Rapture. During college, the panic would set in, and I would quickly seek out anyone who I believed was truly "saved." Most nights, I went to bed, prayed my lucky prayer, and waited for the panic to begin. Some nights, I slept peacefully, but too often, I jolted awake desperately needing to find someone who was "saved." First, I checked the computer lab, then moving on to the TV room, and finally the dorm lobby. Once I found someone more spiritual than I, I slinked back to my bed. In the morning, I covered up my haggard face like the night before never happened. No one else could know that I doubted my salvation or freaked out when the dorm hall was empty. I hid by my good Christian mask as fear gloated over my defeat.

Fear lived alongside me. In the dorm, in class, in every part of my life, fear increased and expanded its icy fingers to clutch any hope or comfort that I still had. Sadly, it thrived in the church, in my faith. Each sermon splayed open my imperfections and my doubts. Sitting in the pew, I wondered if the other church members could see my bruised soul bleeding and strangled by fear. I could never get all of the spiritual disciplines perfected. I believed that once I did everything required in all of the sermons, then I would finally escape my fear. I never could.

Two years after college, I left the church. I broke off all ties with it, its fear-inducing sermons. The pain was too much to carry around from Sunday to Sunday. I'm sure that some church members chalked me up to back-sliding, but it wasn't. I needed to find a place to heal far away from the church. When I left, my fears began leaving too. To most church goers, my radical choice to leave the church would have sent them into fear-induced panic. But I found the chain links that bound me to fear rusting with disuse and breaking down.

As I reflect on my departure from the church, I see that I needed to break all ties with it and its unhealthy cycle of fear. Even my lucky rabbit's foot prayer needed a change. When I prayed it, I focused on the wrong word. I clung to the word "save," but ignored the last word, Jesus. Funny, when I left the church, I found myself drawn more to Jesus not away from Him. Church showed me the way to fear, but Jesus slowly chiseled away my fears replacing them with love. Love freed me. Living in freedom, I don't live in the same panic room, always looking for someone more spiritual or praying to sleep throughout the night. I no longer offer fear a space in my heart.

I wish I could say that once I overcame fear that I ran open-armed to the church. But I can't. I'm still negotiating my path back into fellowship with other Christians. Overcoming fear isn't an easy path nor a smooth one. It doesn't occupy a linear trajectory, and many times, it is full of starts and stops and falling back into fear and getting back out of fear. The process is work, but I promise that it is worth the effort. Today, I feel the last bit of fear fall away, and my faith strengthening. One day, I hope to return to church, but I also choose to guard my new found freedom. It is far too sacred to be destroyed again. In this place, Jesus pushes away my fear, and I can finally believe my lucky prayer—"Save me, Jesus." Because He did.

15

Learning to Let Go

By Alicia Brock

A Dark Winter

"Uh....no... I'm sorry. I'm not interested", I said as I stumbled through the phone conversation with a telemarketer while lying in the fetal position on the couch, as I had been all day. I wouldn't have answered at all, but I was desperately hoping it might be someone calling to offer some relief to my agony. My only prayer that day and the seven days before was for God to please just make the pain stop.

Almost exactly one month earlier, I lost my friend and mentor to cancer. We had prayed for her healing. I was positive God would heal her. She was a beautiful, vibrant young mother of four with so much to offer the world. Of course He would heal her. I had been taught that God desires to give good gifts to his children and that I (as a member of a small church in rural Missouri) was part of God's special chosen people. Since he had so much favor on us, he would not withhold this noble thing we were asking. We were entitled to this kind of miraculous display of divine favor, after all. It wasn't until I watched my friend fight for breath in her last hour of life that I realized my prayers might not be answered.

Over the next month, I would try to comprehend how my friend's death fit in with the dramatic promises "God" had given those of us in this small church. According to the pastor, God was going to make us known worldwide. He was going to pour out his spirit on us in dramatic ways including physical healing. How did we know this? God himself told the pastor, audibly. Over the past two years, "God" had been speaking to the pastor in this way. It was confirmed by God telling secrets about people that no one knew. Our church was small and we considered each other to not just be friends, but true family. We trusted each other. There was no reason to believe our brother would lie to us.

All that changed when my friend died. She was the pastor's wife, and when her illness progressed to the point of no return, he confessed. One month after her death, his confession to two friends would become public. He had not actually heard the audible voice of God, but rather a woman on the leadership team and he had spent countless hours together in private. During this time, he claimed she went into a trance and began speaking as the voice of God. This woman had a savant-like memory for little details no one remembered sharing with her. She used those to confirm the voice was God's and proceeded to control the entire church. Major life decisions had been made based on instructions from this voice and a cult-like bond formed between us all.

This group of people had become the family I always wanted. I loathed my family of origin. When I was a small child I often had daydreams that my life had just been one bad dream and I would wake up and be a baby again. I would be a baby with parents who were able to care for me and I would live in a home that was not constantly swirling with chaos and violence. This church became that family. During my time with them, they built me up and loved on me. During my time with them, my suicidal tendencies ceased. And, because of all this, my bond with them was strong. My identity was entangled with them. My sense of security and wellbeing rested with them. That is, until that one moment.

In that moment, my world came crashing down. My sense of security, identity and family were destroyed. I was deeply betrayed and easily reverted back to the comfort of not trusting. Yet, at the same time, I could not fathom a life without this world that had been created; a world in which I had fully invested myself and helped to create. Those of us who had been equally betrayed found comfort in each other. For a time I was able to hold onto some sense of security as I picked up the pieces and tried to move on.

Glimpses of Spring

Six months later, I met a man. He was genuine, funny, sweet and most of all, he seemed so normal. Right from the beginning, we liked each other. It was as if we were instant best friends. Something inside me knew this relationship felt right. But, I trusted no one, not even myself. Maybe especially myself. After all, I was the one who believed God was speaking audibly to my friend. I had screwed up the last six years of my life following this cult. I clearly was no good judge of character.

While we were dating long distance and I still had the security of my friends, I was able to engage in the relationship without my fears rearing their ugly head too much. But, after six months he asked me leave the only home I had known and move 2000 miles so that we could move forward in our relationship. I had to break up with him, I thought. That's my only option.

As I prepared my breakup speech, I had a crazy thought: "What if....". What if I did go out there? Well, he would spend all his time with his friends and I would be lonely, feel betrayed, we would break up and then I would be all alone with no money, no friends and would end up like Julia Roberts in *Pretty Woman*. The next thought revealed a deeply buried but very real fear. If I go out there, he will realize he doesn't like me all that much, his friends won't like me and most of all, his family will not like me. They will all tell him he shouldn't be with me, he will listen to them and then I will feel betrayed, be all alone with no money or friends and end up like Julia Roberts in *Pretty Woman*. But, it was the thought I had after all these that was the most dangerous. If I go out there and it doesn't work out.... What's really the worst that could happen?

"The worst thing that could happen is that we break up and I move back home and live with my mom until I can save up enough money to move to Colorado and go to graduate school. Oh, that's not so bad. No, actually that's not bad at all. Either way, I am pursuing my dreams and getting out of this crazy hell-hole. Wait, am I crazy for thinking about this?? Crap, I might be." I called my best friend to get a reality check. She reminded me of ways in which my boyfriend had proven his character to me over the last six months and emphatically stated, "That's not the kind of man who is going to bring you out to California and then leave you all alone".

Maybe I *can* do this, I thought. I have a backup plan if it doesn't work out and even Plan B isn't really that bad. At least I can say I tried, right? I called my boyfriend and instead of breaking up, I told him I was in. We were going to start a new life together in California. I felt alive and adventurous. Two months later, I packed the few possessions I hadn't sold in my little Toyota Camry and headed west. I landed in my new town exactly one year after I my world came crashing down, a significant detail I hadn't ignored. I thanked God for redemption, healing and second chances as I drove through mountains and palm trees. My boyfriend and I were off to a great start.

A Long, Dark Night

Fear is a funny thing. Sometimes it is powerful enough to prevent us from moving forward. But, sometimes it is sneaky, like a monster hiding in a closet, and only comes out in full force when the intended target has let their guard down.

It wasn't long after moving to California that my deepest fears began rearing their ugly heads. I scrutinized every move my boyfriend made. I listened intently to every phone call he made and then barraged him with dozens of questions afterward about his relationship with the person on the other end. I searched his computer when he wasn't around for any evidence of him cheating on me and looked through his phone when he was in the bathroom. I called his work on several occasions as an anonymous person to check up on him. I had some awareness that these things were out of the realm of normal, but I was so blinded by my intense fear of being hurt that I couldn't comprehend just how crazy these actions made me look.

I remember one fight we had two weeks after moving there when I announced I was moving back to Missouri. I can't even remember my exact reasons, but I remember that I didn't feel like he had proven to me that he was trustworthy. He said this was a complete shock to him and he had no idea why I was upset or what I was talking about. Somehow he was able to talk me down and convince me to wait a little longer, and I did. However, incidents like these were common. I would often wake up crying, or would cry myself to sleep after allowing thoughts of being betrayed or abandoned to swirl around in my head. I often wondered why he put up with me and my regular outbursts of emotion, but when I wasn't upset, we had a great time together.

This pattern of good times followed by a major meltdown continued for the next several months and followed us as I decided to pursue my dream of living in Colorado. We made a mutual decision to both move to Denver and continue our relationship. Once I arrived there, my issues only increased since he was still working in California and commuting to Denver on his days off. I felt completely alone and abandoned without any friends and without the person who had become my one source of support.

I slipped into a severe depression often hiding in my room after work eating chocolate donuts for dinner, drowning out the pain with TV and then crying myself to sleep. I desperately wanted to experience emotional intimacy, but my fear was paralyzing. My boyfriend began expressing more and more concern for me as I would often unleash all of my emotional turmoil on him through angry and paranoid phone calls and text messages. I was out of control, and I knew it. Somehow, over the next few months, my fear of losing my boyfriend transformed. Instead of losing him in an act of betrayal, I was now afraid he would leave me because of my erratic behavior. I decided to get help.

Waiting for Daylight

I sought out the help of a professional counselor and desperately prayed that my boyfriend would be patient enough to wait and see if things changed. Thank God, he was. As I processed the acts of betrayal of trust in my family and in the church, many of my fears began to cease. I also began to ask my boyfriend to take some extra steps to be more transparent with me in order to build my trust, and then I made a conscious choice to let go of my fears in small increments. I was terrified to let go of my fears, but even more terrified to be alone. I knew this was the only way to save the relationship. Over time, I began to see him for the person he truly is: a kind, loyal man of good character.

The Emergence of Summer

My boyfriend, who I now call "husband", is an airline pilot. Ironically, being married to a pilot requires that there be an immense amount of trust in the relationship. Some say God puts people together not for our happiness but for our holiness: that couples are divinely matched based on strengths and weaknesses so they can help refine each other. I don't know if this is true, but I do know that as broken human beings, we all have fears and those fears are bound to collide when two people engage in relationship with one another. Just as our fears are caused and provoked by relationships, they can also be healed by relationships if we are truly willing to face them. Those years when I was driven by fear and insecurity were horribly painful. But, they taught me that facing my fear does not mean I will be consumed by it. It is the only way to overcome it.

The early years of our relationship seem like a distant memory. The pain I experienced as my life in Missouri came to a screeching halt seems like a bad dream. And as I sit curled up on the same couch I lay in seven years ago, enveloped in the warmth and safety of my husband's arms, I feel as if my life is a dream from which I never want to be awaken.

16

The Spirit of Fear

By Travis Mamone

As I wonder exactly how I'm going to begin this story, I realize something: I'm afraid. I'm afraid that my story won't make any sense. I'm afraid that no one is going to be able to relate to me. I'm afraid that it's going to end up reading like a crappy teenage diary. Should I even bother writing this story?

It's always the same thing.

I missed so many childhood milestones because of my fears. I never learned to swim because I am afraid of drowning. I've never been on a rollercoaster because I'm scared of heights. I don't have a lot of close friends because I'm afraid to talk to people. No matter where I go, fear is always there, following me like a shadow.

Some of my past fears have been pretty stupid, to be honest. In elementary school I used to be scared of fire drills. It wasn't the actual sound itself that bothered me; it was the fact that at any moment, when all is quiet and calm, the shrill screech of a fire drill could rip through the silence and make me jump out of my seat. As soon as I hit middle school, though, fire drills no longer bothered me.

Then there was the time I was afraid of Pink Floyd. Yes, you read right: I used to be afraid of one of my favorite bands! On my twelfth birthday I received "The Wall" album as a gift. The music was so theatrical, the lyrics were so dark, and Gerald Scarfe's album sleeve illustrations were so weird that I thought I was actually listening to some one's nervous breakdown. Years later "The Wall" ended up being one of my all-time favorite albums, and the movie with Bob Geldof is one of my all-time favorite movies.

As I got older my silly fears about fire drills and prog-rock gave way to more serious concerns—like the end of the world.

The first time it happened, I was seventeen and found a book at the library about Nostradamus and end-time prophecy. At first I didn't really pay much attention, since this was the spring of 2000 and the Y2K catastrophe didn't happen. But then I wondered, "What if it was true?" And since I had no way of knowing what was going to happen, I thought about the apocalypse more and more. By the time summer came, I couldn't enjoy my vacation because I was convinced that I was living in the shadow of the apocalypse. I would lie in bed and shiver, thinking about the world being swallowed up in a big ball of fire. Eventually those fears passed, but they resurfaced in 2006 when I came across a book called The Bible Code that claimed that a nuclear war was going to occur that August. Of course, that didn't happen either, and I wasted another summer paralyzed by fear.

I don't really fear the end the world anymore. Instead, my fears are focused on every day things: money, relationships, jobs, the future, and all of the good stuff that comes with being an adult. One might say, "But Travis, everyone has those worries." True, except that my anxiety isn't just your normal everyday nervousness, like giving a big presentation in front of all your co-workers.

For me, anxiety is like being in thrown into a lions' den, like Daniel in the Bible. Even though I'm nervous at first, I quickly tell myself, "I know how this story ends. The lions won't eat me." The guards seal the mouth of the den shut, and the lions slowly creep towards me, licking their lips. I wait patiently as the lions get closer. They start smelling and licking me. "Okay, God," I think, "you can come and save me now." One of the lions gently nibbles on my arm, the way a cat does, except I can't tap a lion on the head and say, "Bad kitty!" I slowly back away from the lions, but they move closer. I climb up a rock as they paw me, scratching up my legs in the process. I pound on the rock covering the mouth of the den and scream, "For God's sake, get me out of here! I was wrong about the whole 'God's going to save me' thing, okay? Hello? Is anybody there? Get me out!"

I know that God doesn't give us the spirit of fear, but I honestly think He made an exception with me. Why else would I constantly be afraid of every single mishap that might happen throughout the day? I try being optimistic, but every time I think things are going to be okay, something happens and my whole day is shot to hell. So I've learned to live in a constant state of fear, that way I'll always be ready for the next big catastrophe. And if that next big catastrophe never happens, at least I can say I was prepared just in case.

Living in fear gets tiring after a while, though. It takes a lot of energy and willpower to be so tense and nervous all the time. Some days I feel I don't have enough energy to get out of bed in the morning. Eventually I get so tired that I have to go after the source of all my fears: God.

I yell and scream at God for all the shit He puts me through. I curse Him up and down, left and right, and every other direction I can think of. “You like seeing me suffer, don’t you? Why should I give you praise? You ain’t never done shit for me!” And then, when my voice is shot from all the screaming, I hear a still small voice in my head saying, “That wasn’t Me you were screaming at. That’s some other god.”

Maybe God is trying to give me a spirit of peace, but I just can’t accept it. After all, if I can’t live my life in absolute fear, what else am I supposed to do? But maybe this “spirit of peace” thing might not be so bad after all, so I’ll give it a try.

17

Conquered by a Sneeze

By Misty Chaffins

My fear was conquered by a sneeze.

But that's the end of the story. It all started with two pink lines. I felt the steely fingers grip my heart. I was 22 and unmarried. I wasn't even technically dating the guy...we were the "on again-off again" couple. We loved each other, but we were young and not done sowing our wild oats. Until now. Rich was a musician and had dreams of the big time. This was going to change everything.

He came over to my place that night and I showed him the stick that said, "You are going to be parents." His next words will live in infamy: "Guess we're going to be friends for a long time, huh?"

As if it wasn't obvious, Rich wasn't ready to become a dad. So, he continued on his path to fame and away from me. I was completely terrified as well, but I couldn't quite run from the pregnancy like he did. I kept him in the loop, but I was scared. I had always wanted to be a mother. There is absolutely nothing like the feeling of holding a sleeping baby in your arms and I couldn't wait for the baby to be mine. Then there were times that I couldn't breathe because I didn't know how I was going to make life work being on my own and having a baby, but I couldn't continue to be back and forth like this. I was already feeling very protective of my baby. He deserved better. Fortunately, Rich felt the same way. When I was about 5 months along in my pregnancy, he proposed.

My pregnancy was going very well, and it felt like life was complete. We decided that we didn't want to know what we were having since there are so few genuine surprises in this world anymore. So we chose a boy and a girl name, Christian Wesley or Kristen Emory, and called it Baby Chris for short. We got the wedding planned and I was 7 months along when we walked down the aisle feeling baby Chris kicking to join in the ceremony. I moved to North Carolina with him and set out to build our lives. Everything was going wonderfully.

I found a really nice doctor and was going to deliver in a smaller hospital in the area. This was a faith-based hospital and I loved that idea. I really wanted a home birth but since I had never done this before, I was opting for at least a natural birth. I was terrified, but felt like She-Ra. Things were great and only getting better.

I had gained a good bit of weight. I guess that's what you get for being stuck at home with no friends for 2 months. My blood pressure was a little higher than they wanted it to be and I had pre-eclampsia So, six days before my due date, my doctor decided to help things along and stripped my membranes. I started having some light contractions in the afternoon. We had our last childbirth class that evening and by then, I was having some time-able contractions. They were coming every 5 minutes and were uncomfortable, but bearable. I was beyond excited to have this baby. But I was treading into the unknown and nervous. We went to the hospital about 10 that evening, but was sent home and told to go see my doctor in the morning or come back if my water broke. About 1 am my water broke. Time to go have a baby!

Unfortunately, hard and fast contractions started immediately and I couldn't even dress myself to go. We got things together and I made it as far as the porch with I started throwing up. I was ready for an epidural right now. No one had told me about this part. We finally made it to the hospital and my visions of walking and laboring in different positions were dashed, my blood pressure was so high that I was only allowed to lie on my left side. I was pretty disappointed. This isn't how it was supposed to go and I was losing control of the situation. I was asking for an epidural, but they didn't want to give it to me too early. I don't remember much of this time except for lying there riding the waves of the contractions. I was scared and felt like I was a failure because things were not going like I had planned.

They checked me when they thought I should be about 4 cm dilated (their magic number for the epidural) but I was actually twice that. In very little time, I was fully dilated and ready to push. I was so tired and this was hard work! No matter how hard I pushed, he just wouldn't come. He was stuck on my pubic bone. They tried the forceps and the vacuum, but he just was too big. His heart rate started dropping in between contractions, and that's when they decided that it was time to get this baby born and we headed to the OR to have a c-section. I just wanted to have him in my arms already. Things progressed normally at this point and Rich got to see Christian Wesley born weighing in at a beautiful 8 lbs 4 oz.

They took him to the corner to get him cleaned up and do all the normal stuff, but I didn't hear him cry. I started asking the anesthesiologist what was wrong, why couldn't I hear him crying. I was starting to panic. He has to cry! It took a few minutes, but they finally told me that he hadn't started breathing on his own and they had to put a tube down his throat to help him breath. My world just turned upside down. I had to remind myself to breathe. My baby, my perfect baby. Rich was back at my side holding my hand and we just looked at each other in shock. They continued to work on both of us while most of the people in the room came over to pray for him with us. I couldn't think. It was just like a vacuum had opened up under me. I had still not seen my baby. He couldn't be taken from me when I hadn't even seen him yet.

They finished with me and took me out to the recovery area. Rich was going back and forth from the waiting area, to me, and then to check on Christian. They informed us that they were going to transfer him to a larger hospital equipped to handle sick babies. As the neonatal team took Christian out to the ambulance for the transfer, I finally got my first look. He was absolutely beautiful. Perfect. He had started having seizures by then and it looked like he was waving to me. I had no idea if this would be the last time I got to see my baby alive and I could barely breathe.

So many things going through my head. What had I done wrong? How could this be happening? Dear God, please just let my baby live and be ok. I will do anything. I was a shell of a person, a part of me had just been taken away.

Later, we got a call from the doctor that was caring for our little guy. He told us that things were not good, but he was stable for now. We pinned all our hopes on that. They decided to transfer me so I could be closer to Christian. After I got there, I was asking to go see him. I wasn't going to let the c-section keep me away from him. My baby boy looked like a giant compared to all the tiny premies in the NICU. He still looked just perfect. My heart swelled just looking at him. I wanted to scoop him up and love him but we weren't allowed to touch him because of over stimulation. They had stopped the seizures, but his brain was still very fragile. I finally got to hold him the next day. My perfect baby was finally in my arms, I felt complete again. Now if he would just open his eyes and look at me.

The doctors were tactful, but didn't give us any false hope. Christian stayed stable for the next two days while we clung to the smallest scrap of hope that we could find. I sat with him while holding his hand and praying for him to wake up. I sang lullabies to him. I was his mother, he needed me to be strong, he needed me to fight for him. If only my will could overcome whatever was trying so desperately to take him away. But I lived those days in fear. Fear of the unknown and "what might be". Fear that what I was doing wasn't enough, that I wasn't a good enough mother to keep him with me. That I might have to let go. That fear came to light when Christian spiked a fever and it became obvious that he was too sick to stay with us. The doctors started preparing us for the worst. We spent the next two days holding him as much as we could and trying to memorize every tiny feature on his face. I wanted him to leave this world knowing that we loved him more than anything. So many tears were shed. I was devastated. My perfect little boy was only going to be in my arms for a very short while. I would never get to sit and rock him while watching those beautiful eyes close in sleep. All I could think about was all the things I would never be able to tell him or do with him. I couldn't see how I was ever going to feel whole again.

When it was time, they took all the wires from him except his breathing tube and we got to bathe him and dress him, then we had a little ceremony where he was baptized. The nurse removed his tube while Rich and I both held him and kissed him. Then our angel flew to God after being with us for only 5 days.

I don't remember much of the next several days. I know that I slept a lot. When I was awake, it felt like I was in a well made of glass. People were near but I couldn't touch them, I could see them but not really hear them. What I remember most about this time was the physical ache in my arms. I was supposed to be holding and cuddling my baby, but they were empty and nothing could fill them.

It was this reason that I wanted to try for another baby right away. Not to replace Christian, nothing could do that. Just to fill my aching arms. Even though I made it my mission to get pregnant immediately, it took almost a year. Right before what would have been Christian's first birthday, I found out that I was pregnant again. I breathed a sigh of relief, but almost immediately the fear struck. What if I miscarry? What if there are problems with the delivery again? What if I lose this baby too? Could I live through that again?

There was always trepidation about this pregnancy. Ladies who meant well would share their wonderful birth stories while fear had my heart in its grip. I began to believe some of the things that fear whispered. I was not meant to be a mother, I wasn't eating/sleeping/exercising right. Then they started to be about more than just the baby. That I was a weak and insignificant person. My whole world revolved around fear. I couldn't make a move without thinking and rethinking my options. I started feeling panicked and closed in. Then we decided that we wanted everything to be different this time in hopes that the outcome would be different. I started eating healthier. I stayed away from any medications. Unfortunately, things began to look very familiar. I started having blood pressure problems and was placed on bed rest. We were having another little boy, and the resemblance continued.

On my 25th birthday, the doctors decided to deliver him 2 weeks early due to the pre-eclampsia. I got my epidural and was wheeled into the OR while listening to the doctors talk about staying up late to watch the crazy election results from the day before. They still hadn't been sure who won, Bush or Gore. I was shouting in my head that it didn't matter, didn't they understand? How could they talk about something so mundane when my whole life was about to change and I had no idea which way it was going to tip. With Rich by my side, we faced the unknown yet again, but with our eyes open. We could see both sides of the veil. I was jealous of the people that went to the hospital with the absolute certainty that they would be leaving in a few day's time with an infant in their arms. I longed for that peace but I could never be that naive again.

"Ok, there is going to be some pressure."

What I heard next was like nothing I have ever heard again. It was a tiny little sneeze. My heart was released of that terrible fear. He was breathing and beautiful!

With him in my arms and Rich by my side, I was able to look at the fear and all the lies that came with it and really see how much I had accomplished. I hadn't let that fear paralyze me and keep me from the family that I so longed for. The Bible tells us that perfect love casts out fear, and I have seen those words come alive in my life.

18

Harbor Me

By Jen Rose

Gold ribbons of sun filter through the trees on this drive down County Road 44. It's a two-lane highway through not-quite-rural towns, lined with dense, forever green trees that wear misty cloaks in the morning light. Some Sundays, especially when the traffic is light and the air is cool, I believe I could drive this stretch a few times and call it an act of worship. Air whooshes through rolled-down windows, circling the inside of the car and rushing back out, disrupting my hair along the way. It doesn't matter how messy my hair is for church. It only speaks to the mess I feel inside.

Could I make a confession? Few Sundays go by that I don't consider turning around and going back. Almost thirty minutes in the car is long enough to let the voices of doubt, insecurity, and confusion fight for the upper hand. No matter what my outside routine shows, I can agree with them on one point. Yes, I am a misfit soul dressed in a patchwork faith. Yes, I love and am loved, but sometimes I am so afraid.

***

As far back as I remember, I never quite fit in. Quiet and plain, my world was within, my imaginative country as wide as the ocean that surrounds the sandy land of my birth. Between the high concentration of theme parks and the spray-tanned spring break transients, Florida is a state of make-believe, and perhaps growing up in its mixed-up culture helped me become good at pretending. My sister and I were nurtured by the colorful creatures of Dr. Seuss, then we graduated to after-school Disney cartoons and hours devoted to mastering Super Mario World. In our play, we embellished the stories we knew with our own characters and subplots, creating with the wild abandon only children seem to have.

Recently, I read that a lack of imagination is the biggest roadblock to our theology, and I can believe it. At any age it takes a child's vision to see God clearly enough to believe in him. I was baptized at six years old by a preacher I don't remember on a day that seems long ago, simply because believing in the God of my parents made sense. A good decade later, it all became real to me as I cried over my open Bible and these words: "But he was pierced for our transgressions... and by his wounds we are healed." (Isaiah 53:5 -- NIV) To first see the world through the eyes of the suffering servant was a grace. The words spoke to a deep need I couldn't name and connected the dots between my head and heart. They said I was dirty and loved and God himself became man and let man break him so I could be clean. So there I was, fourteen, at the height of 90s evangelicalism and the WWJD phenomenon, with a fire and a passion to make sure everybody knew about the incredible story I'd stumbled into.

I made a promise to God there. Sorry God. I'll do better. Pray more. Read the Bible all the time. Wear Christian t-shirts so people knew which team I played for. I spent hours in Bible study and listened only to Christian music. My first published writing was a rebuttal to a local paper's editorial titled "Religion is the Problem." And I wrote poems, lots of them, all about God, salvation, and how great it would be to die for my faith. My pen was a dagger I brandished to defend the Lion of Judah printed so on my oversized glow-in-the-dark-at-the-skating-rink T-shirt.

How fearless I was. Lion-hearted as I felt though, there was this sneaking, lurking insecurity that I wasn't enough. I never "led anyone to Christ" or went on a mission trip, and never fully plugged into a youth group. I could barely talk to anyone my age. I thrived as a homeschooler and joined a deep Bible study with my mom, but whenever I tried to make friends at homeschool groups or classes, I turned small, inward, and tongue-tied. It would be years before I learned this just meant I was an introvert. At the time, I wondered if it meant something was wrong with me.

Once, I wore faith like a new trim and tailored coat. Oh, how I took pride in it, polishing the buttons until I could see my sparkling reflection, tightening the warmth around me, impervious to the coldest wind and rain. It was conservative and timeless, and if it had a color it would be no-nonsense navy blue, without a stray hair or shred of lint on the surface. I wore it with pride. It was the only one in my wardrobe, so gracious a gift in exchange for filthy rags.

But over time, all things become rags. And when it's the only coat you've got, you have to patch the holes with what you find.

There was the time I went to a charismatic church with the guy that had a crush on me. I pulled some threads from that, glittery gold and passionate purple, and stitched up the hole stuffy religion had made. They danced, they reveled, they felt! But feeling isn't all, and I found my shy self unable to join the dance.

When college introduced me to a storm of new ideas that threatened to unravel the edges, studying the Emergent movement gave me some faint chiffon to trim them up. I became more comfortable with abstract thought, and something in their embrace of community, love, and unanswered questions whispered reality to me. I searched online for a church that fit the profile, but found no signs of such a place near me. But would I, with my inward-turning, even fit with such a community-focused life? And even if I did, would it satisfy the part of me that liked to think? Still, the airy colors suited for a while.

Where Emergence spoke to my artist's love of abstraction, there was still a part of me that longed for firm direction. When several of my friends became Reformed, I found myself immersed in their world, and I admired their confidence, passion, and freedom. Sturdy and thick, their doctrines took care of the holes college wore in the elbows, but still, there were so many details that were hard to swallow. I could see the beauty of tradition and an unchanging God with total control, but the more I followed the trail of logic, the more confused I became.

And so it goes, stealing scraps of everything from dowdy fundamentalist Baptist skirts to patches from Christian rock shows to ancient scraps that smell of liturgical incense and ash, all attempts to mend the holes in my fraying coat. Underneath is a small soul -- frail, naked, and afraid -- wrapped in something more like dirty old patchwork than anything. If this were taken away, if doubt-moths ate through it and exposed me as an impostor, would I have anything left? Would I die of exposure?

Here I am still, afraid of not fitting in, not knowing my place -- a childish fear to some, but one that never fully goes away in many of us. Sometimes I believe I'm not good enough to call myself a Christian. I feel fake. I feel like God and I barely speak, like Jesus is the Facebook friend I keep around but never talk to. I compare myself and come up short, because I don't speak in super-happy Christianese, because I doubt, because I sometimes barely find the words to pray beyond the Lord's Prayer, help me, and thank you. I'm afraid to even write it out and risk exposure.

But somehow, I believe when we name our fears for the monsters they are, we can control them, we can fight them. I've heard it said that sometimes when we sin, when we doubt or fall away, it's less because we want to do wrong and more because we forgot who we belong to. When I pull my patchwork faith around me, shivering and crying "It's not enough!" and "Why won't you help me?" it's a comfort that I have faith enough to call for help. I look at the ones that seem so much better, the golden boys and perfect girls, and wonder if maybe, just maybe, they're as prodigal as I am, holding their own patches together too.

***

That day I was despairing on the way to church, asking God why he didn't speak to me anymore, why I felt like an abandoned child. I drove the rest of the trip and dragged myself inside. My church isn't in a trendy warehouse, abandoned theater, quaint country building, or sumptuous cathedral. It looks like any other church I would have gone to in the past, small enough to have a vague idea of who people are, but big enough that I can fake invisibility when I need to.

I sat in the old pew and noticed something about the people around me. We are a rather patchwork group ourselves. There are bikers and hippies, rednecks and nerds, lovely young families and elderly women with bright lips and bold dresses. We look like a family of misfits, all adopted and beautiful, slightly dysfunctional. Some shout "Praise the Lord" in greeting and mean it. Others dig daily for the hope to carry on.

This day, we learned a new song, "Love You Swore," and our leader sang it like he needed reassurance as much as I did. And with every verse, my soul lifted, just a little.

"I know that I love you, but sometimes I am afraid."[1]

Someday, we will all be changed. Our faith becomes sight; our dirty rags and patchwork jobs that keep us barely clothed will be burned away. And we will have new names, new garments shining like the sun.

Imagine that. Burning, white-hot souls with the dust and dirt of fear washed away by love.

"Harbor me in the eye of the storm.

I'm holding on to the love you swore."

What else is there to hold? I pull my coat around me and rest safely in the shelter, waiting for the clouds to break.

---

1 John Mark McMillan. "Love You Swore." *Economy.* Integrity Music, 2011.

19

Embracing My Singleness in the Church

By Juan M. Guerra

It will be three years in April of this year when I started attending a non-denominational Christian church in the Peninsula of the Bay Area with my best friend, Jose. He extended an invitation to me when I was ready to experience God on a different level. I was afraid of visiting the church because I didn't want to experience anything that I thought was out of the ordinary. And I was afraid of attending church as a single man because I didn't want to be judged. The idea of ending up alone and not having a woman I could share my life with frightened me. I had a girlfriend between elementary to junior high and I truly believed she was my soul mate. When we separated in the summer before freshman year of high school, fear had come into existence and lowered my confidence level. I was rejected many times and I feared I would never find a girl that had similar personality traits to my past girlfriend. But because I was relying on my own understanding and not trusting in the Lord, I became lost in a field of wandering sheep. I did, however, prayed to God to give me an answer about living a single life. I wanted to seek Him and understand why I was in a situation that gave me fear of being single.

On January 16, 2011, God answered my prayer after nine months. That particular sermon was on the subject of single people and married couple. *Stay Single if You Can; Get Married if You Must* - what a fitting title for a sermon! This was no mere coincidence. It was God's perfect timing to let me know He was looking out for me and had orchestrated Jose and I to go together that morning to understand each other's view points on singleness and married couple. I saw this opportunity as an answered prayer.

Strike One: Integrating Singles in the church

After a moment of prayer and worship, our lead pastor dived into the book of 1 Corinthians 7. In it, Apostle Paul discusses the issue of singleness and marriage, spiritual gifts and our calling to serve God. Throughout the service I tried to understand marriage and how Jose was going through that journey with his wife. Then God threw a perfectly curve ball in my direction as our pastor moved on to single people and their role in the church. He acknowledged the fact that the church needed to integrate singles in the full fellowship of the church.

> "If you're single, get into other ministries, serve and pray with people. Don't isolate yourself. For those of you who are married, do whatever you can to make sure there are open doors for singles in your group and in your family."

Confirmation! A huge grin spread across our faces. Jose and I had a previous conversation about how he and his family had 'adopted' me as a new member of the family. God was definitely working through the pastor.

Strike Two: Forge A Special Relationship

The pastor went on to explain how his own family has had the joy and privilege over the years to call many single adults their best friends. "They forge a unique and special relationship with our kids that I am so grateful," he exclaimed with joy.

Jose and his family took me under their wing, welcomed me into their home, and made me feel that I belonged. They also allowed me to be an 'uncle' to their five-year-old daughter who is absolutely smart, funny, adorable and loves Jesus with all her heart. I have come to realize that God has blessed me with an amazing group of friends who have become a second family to me that I can count on. I feel the love that surrounds me when I spend time with them.

Strike Three: Embracing Your Calling and Gifts

For those of you who are still single; how do you know if being single is a calling, or a gift from God? What God taught me is that if being single isn't hard for you, and if you generally like where you are in that moment of your life, then you probably have that gift. The calling we have often fits with what we do well and what we enjoy. Many of us are called to things that aren't easy for us. Moses was called to lead Israel out of Egypt, but he didn't feel like that was a good fit for him at all. We should learn to embrace our single life and trust that God will lead us the way in His perfect timing. God is all about love and unity.

Homerun!

I can honestly say I was afraid to live the single life, but because I committed my life to Jesus Christ, my life changed and transformed in a radical way because of who He is. I was told my Christian faith would be challenged once I had chosen to be on Team Jesus, but I never imagined how it would really take over if I let it. I trust God with all my heart and soul He will provide a woman into my life. And Maybe He won't, but it's not for me to decide or control. I do know having an intimate relationship with Jesus will mature my faith and equip me with the shield God promises us in time of battles.

I'm not afraid. Through all of these experiences and growing as a Christian, I have learned to fear God in a way I never thought possible. I am obedient to Him because I know He has something radical and magazine for every one of us on this earth. My fear of being a single man in church has been diminished and in no hurry to be in a relationship. I am enjoying the way my life is right now and when I feel it's time to find that woman in my life then I will act on doing my part and praying that God guides me on my journey. I can truly tell you I am excited to see what God has in store for me. He's always throwing curve balls to keep us on our toes, and let me tell you - He's a fast one!

"Trust in the Lord with all your heart and not lean on your own understanding." - Proverbs 3:5

20

Faith in Fear

By Daryl Thomson

We sat across from each other. He in his brown sweater and brown shoes. Me in my warn denim and grey, flannel hoodie. My chair was a throwback to the 1960s – thick aluminum tubing wrapped around an unforgiving red plastic seat. The stark silence between us spoke volumes about my reluctance to engage as well as my deep yearning for someone to finally listen to me.

The old, electric clock on the wall hummed.

He clicked his pen and started to doodle on the back of a scrap piece of blue paper. At first it looked like he was sketching a mountain or half an egg or some strange elliptical sun starting to sink below the horizon. But then he turned the paper around so I could see more clearly.

He had drawn a tombstone.

> "Let's pretend for a moment that you get hit by a bus tomorrow," he said. "No, let's pretend that you get hit by a bus on the way home today and that you

> don't make it. You're done. Finished. It's all over. Based on how and where you see yourself, what do you think would be the most fitting epitaph that sums up your life to this point?"

I looked at him blankly wondering if I should play along with his perverse interpretation of Pictionary or if I should try to bluster my way out of responding. I was fragile. I was still in recovery. The longer I remained motionless, the more awkward it became. So to humor him, I picked up my pen and started to reflect.

Only a few seconds passed before the unexpected tsunami of emotion came ashore. I never even heard the warning siren. I was swept up in one of those moments when self awareness comes crashing through the levees of self-protection and pride leaving only the raw, exposed truth. I knew right away what to write – what I had to write. And it crushed me.

Me – the one who had big dreams of even bigger adventures.

Me – the one who was once full of confidence and courage.

Me – the optimist, the wide-eyed, big-hearted believer that anything was possible.

I picked up his pen and wrote four simple but tragic words to summarize my perspective of the journey thus far:

"This Wasn't Really Me"

As I wrote my own epitaph on my cartoon gravestone, I was sad. Deeply sad. Because somewhere along the way, this world-changer, adventurer, pioneer, and free spirit had grown small and afraid. Afraid of making the wrong choice, afraid of failure, afraid that his dreams weren't worth anything anymore, afraid of starting because he couldn't see the finish, afraid of living for fear of dying. And I knew this to be true deep in my bones this because only three short months prior, I almost died.

It was a sunny afternoon in September – a Tuesday to be exact – and I thought I would take the opportunity to enjoy a quick noontime run. I had been training for a half marathon all summer and so the thought of running for half an hour seemed like a treat compared to the almost two hours I logged the Sunday before. I changed from my work clothes into my running gear, plugged in my iPod, tightened my laces and headed out.

Exactly twelve minutes later I was on the ground - gasping, groaning, clutching my hand to my chest, and growing more frightened by the moment. Once the pain started to radiate into my lower left arm and wrist, I knew what was happening. I knew I was having a heart attack. I knew I was in serious trouble because I wasn't anywhere convenient where help could reach me. I thought I was going to die. No fanfare. No heroic martyrdom. Just an average man who had led an average life, worked an average job, and had an average amount of faith.

From the outside, I was healthy. I don't smoke. I don't drink excessively. I'm not diabetic. I was under forty years old at the time and had been running significant distances for years without any problems. So to find myself being wheeled into the cardiac ward where two stents would be inserted into a blocked coronary artery was terrifying, destabilizing, and bewildering.

In the months of recovery following the heart attack, I spent long hours alone in my living room, faced with the acute reality of my own mortality and asking the big questions:

Why am I still here?

For what purpose have I been created?

And, perhaps most importantly: Am I content to live with average or is there something more?

My friends and family listened patiently as I wrestled with these questions – sometimes getting brief moments of clarity and sometimes sinking into swamps of hopelessness. At times, they cried with me as I poured out my brokenness, frustration, and grief over wanting to live beyond the average but being too afraid to transform dreams into reality. At other times they encouraged me to take a risk, to have faith in faith, and to start living the life I could only dream of. As I sat on my couch, paralyzed by the internal tension of desperately wanting to live a life of significance but fearful of the steps to move in that direction, I prayed, I cried, I screamed, and I sulked.

I was afraid. And the irony is the fears that surfaced during my recovery felt like they were slowly killing my spirit and soul far more effectively than any heart attack could have. I hated my fear-induced paralysis. I grew despondent about having to return to a life that was only adequately fulfilling and labor at a job that was safe – safe but not soul enriching. I wanted to either find the courage to break free from the invisible chains of so-called security and stability or else find a way to choke the life from the part of my soul that longed for something more.

I have grown into adulthood believing that the opposite of fear is courage, where courage is the power to see clearly into uncomfortable or unknown situations and advance instead of retreat – or remain stationary. But as I have grappled with my own fears, I am starting to wonder if the opposite of fear is not courage, but faith. Courage is momentary and situational in that specific moments call forth demonstrations of courage in both public and private ways. But faith is an ever-present posture that may wax or wane in intensity but that guides through all of life's events. Courage may be needed for a sprint, but faith wins marathons.

I have discovered that fear is a thief and a liar and hates to be exposed so I have begun to put specific names to my fears. I am trying to see myself no longer as a fearful person, but instead as one who is afraid of specific things. I am afraid of failure. I am afraid of suffering. I am afraid of having too much and I am afraid of having too little. Although fear still exists, naming it allows me to drag it out of the shadows and into the sunlight where it can be examined, observed, and confronted.

My journey out of fear is slow and awkward and although I have taken steps to begin moving in directions that reflect an emerging sense of identity and calling, the cold shadow of fear still hovers close. At times, my list of fears is long and troubling, but naming my fears at least gives me a fighting chance to break free from their spell and realize that all is not hopeless. I can still dream. I can still embrace new experiences and integrate them into the constantly emerging mosaic that is me. I can still affirm and declare life because of an emerging awareness that faith is more powerful than fear.

When fear whispers in my ear that running into change and chasing after dreams are mere folly, faith reassures me that it is safe to step outside of convention. When fear mocks my fragile capacity for hope, faith nurtures hope like a newly planted seedling – sustaining, feeding, and protecting from that which would see it wither and die. And when fear places my past on trial in order to condemn my future, faith unlocks the prison doors of failure, self-doubt and uncertainty and sets me free.

21

Questionable Beauty

By Lore Ferguson

It happened when I was nine, a skinny fourth grader, mousy brown hair and a stubborn soul. I don't know what I was told to wear that morning, but I know what I wore because it is there, memorialized in color, on a 5x7 school photo. Glasses were new to me and I had picked out blue plastic frames; it was the 80s, but still? I wore a patterned blue shirt, blue shorts, sandals with blue socks. I thought this meant I matched.

When the photos came, as they did every year, in a big white envelope, I stared back at the face staring at me and that's when it happened. That's when I knew what I was sure everyone must have known all along: *I was ugly*.

It was the comparison of the girls beside me, their hair in ribbons and their pretty plaid dresses, pressed and flounced. It was the realization that my hair would never be sleek and shiny, or blond. It was the truth that my features would always be bigger or smaller, while the features of other girls would always be more beautiful, more feminine, more *anything* than what I could ever be. It was a belief that I've carried with me my entire life: I'm ugly. Maybe someday I'll be a swan, but today, I'm the ugly duckling.

So when my roommate asks me to resolve to love my body this year, its nuances and its curves, its imperfections and its perfectly crafted parts, I balk. I can't do that. Loving others comes oh so naturally to me, loving myself is always a resolution for *next* year.

When a friend asks me to write a blog on whether looks matter in relationships, I tell him that I'm probably the last person to write that blog.

When I have a conversation with a friend and I'm talking about the doubt in my soul regarding so many things related to looks (mine and others), she stops me and says, "What are you afraid of?"

What am I afraid of?

I'm afraid of two things: the first is that I'll find what is *not* beautiful to be beautiful; the second is that I'll never be found beautiful.

So I want to know, really, what is beautiful? And does it matter what is beautiful?

WHAT IS BEAUTY?

I say it often enough about nearly every person I know, every piece of art in my home, the spate of days we've been having in Texas, the sunsets that make me gasp, the conversations I have with friends; it is never difficult for me to find beauty in every single thing I know. I'm prone to finding beauty in so many things that my friends just roll their eyes now when another exclamation comes from my mouth.

But what is beauty outside the eye of the beholder?

What is beauty when it can be teased apart from shiny magazine spreads and museum walls and computer screens in a midnight bedroom? What is beauty when it is seen through the lens of the gospel and nothing less?

I only know to start with the fact that Jesus spent his earthly time and energy teaching us to turn a kingdom of classes into a kingdom of completion. His interest was in the poorest, the lowest, the outcast, *and* the richest, the most corrupt, the most beautiful. This morning my pastor spoke how Christ came to reconcile us to Himself and us to one another, but what most struck me is that Christ came to reconcile *us to ourselves.*

Ourselves.

Myself.

My self.

IMAGO DEI

Self love is not a topic I want to talk about when I think about beauty. Here's why: I want all the beautiful people to start loving the unbeautiful. I want the perfect people to start loving the imperfect, the unlovely. I want there to be an impact that is measurable, *tangible*, and I don't know that self-love is the most productive way of getting there.

But here is the argument I'd like to make: if we do not love the self we have been given, we are exercising ungratefulness toward the God who created us in His image. We are, in essence, rejecting God who dwells in our temporal temples.

And I would add this, when we reject what God has called beautiful in others, even if we ourselves do not find it instantly attractive, we are denying what God has created in them.

When I call that fourth grade photo ugly, I look at the imago dei, the image of God, and I blaspheme what He has called good.

When I look with a critical eye at the mirror tonight while I wash my face and brush my teeth, I blaspheme what He has called good.

Hear me when I say that simply because God has called it good does not mean it has not been broken by the fall. It has, and this is my great, great comfort on days when I feel the curse of having the body of a woman and all the lovely things that entails in particular times of the month.

There is a brokenness that accompanies us wherever we go, hanging on to our backs like a trained monkey. But sometimes we chain that monkey to our own back, buying magazines, feasting our eyes on what is even more broken, in hopes that we can attain what? *More* brokenness?

DO LOOKS MATTER?

Yes. Oh yes they do. Praise God they do. Praise God that He put us here on earth with a garden to tend and pray to Him that we tend it well. Pray that we tend our own plot well and pray that we are attentive to the plots of others. Praise Him that He created different sizes and shapes and colors and genders. Praise Him for His creativity in design. Praise Him that we find anything lovely at all.

Paul says "Whatever is *true*, whatever is *honorable*, whatever is *just*, whatever is *pure*, whatever is *lovely*, whatever is *commendable*, if there is any excellence, if there is anything worthy of praise, *think about these things*." God help us to find beauty wherever we find these things. If we do, we will find that beauty is found readily.

DO LOOKS MATTER?

No. No, they don't. Not really. Not in the end of the story (which is really just the beginning). No, they don't matter here on earth where we will all either grow bellies or waste away to nothing, where the grey hair eventually goes white or disappears completely, where wrinkles grow exponentially, breasts sag, and strength fails. Beauty is so fleeting, so temporal, a vapor.

Gone.

But, which is more, and *so much more beautiful*, looks don't matter because one day everything that does not glorify the Lord will be purified out of us. Everything. Every sag, every wrinkle, every mark, every love handle--and, ***don't miss this***, each and every perfect nose, every straight tooth, every sculpted muscle, every six-pack abdomen. Every health nut and every couch potato, every beauty queen and every street child. **If it is not proclaiming the majesty of the Only One due glory, it will be consumed by the All Consuming Fire.**

My fourth grade me and my 30 year old me. My best version of me and my worst version of me. My joyful reflection of Him and my mirror's sickening reflection of me. All of it will glorify Him.

THE REAL QUESTION

The question is so much more than *What is Beautiful*? or *Do looks matter*? The question is, am I valuing what God values in me and am I valuing it in others?

No matter what my fourth grade photo instilled in me, He is the standard of my beauty.

The real beauty in that is, because He is the standard, I know I can't ever measure up.

There is nothing good in me but what He has redeemed for His glory, so I am always the ugly duckling who was picked even in my ugliness. He didn't wait for my inner swan to grow. He's not waiting for some future version of me to materialize. He's not waiting for me to match a magazine spread or even grow happy with this earthly version of me. He's after me seeing the depth of what He's done *in* me. *Through* me. *With* me. For His glory. Alone.

He's after me seeing Him in the mirror.

Fear and Your Relationships

Introduction

By Alise Wright

I am surrounded by relationships that I don't fully understand.

In 1997, my best friend from high school came out to me as a lesbian. In 2009, my Christian husband of 13 years told me that he no longer believed in God. In 2010, I realized that my closest relationship was with a married man.

These aren't the kind of relationships that one is supposed to have as a Christian. Perhaps we can be friends with a gay person as long as they know that we think their "lifestyle choices" are not acceptable to God. Perhaps we can be in a relationship with someone of another faith, or even no faith, as long as we are diligently trying to convert them to Christianity. Perhaps we can have a cross-gender friend as long as we are careful to obey all of the rules about how we interact and never get too close to them.

But ultimately, it's probably just best if we have close friends who are just like us. People who conform to our view of what life is supposed to be like. People who look like us and act like us and think like us.

None of the relationships that are closest to me fit into those nice, neat categories. Instead, they break outside of all the boxes and have forced me outside of those boxes as well. I have been made to examine prejudices that I have about people who are different from me. They have forced me to look at myself and determine areas of lack in my life. Sometimes that introspection didn't feel very good. I don't like to see the ways that I write off people based on differences between us. I like to think of myself as a fairly accepting person, but as these relationships have come into my life, I must look at the ways that I choose not to be inclusive, and then decide if my concerns outweigh my desire to love.

Of course, for me, it's about working with the friends that I have. For some, choosing have close relationships at all is a whole other consideration.

For some people, even the prospect of going and talking to someone stirs up all kinds of anxiety for them. Even the person who is like them represents a potential rejection. Better to just stay quiet and hope that someone comes to you.

And let's not even get into families. The people who are likely some of the most formative relationships can also be some of the most complicated. What happens when we don't end up like those in our family of origin? What if those people were abusive and hurtful to us rather than nurturing us and caring for us the way that they were supposed to? How do we navigate the complexities of family relationships with grace and love when sometimes those elements are missing from them? As things change in our families, how do we adapt to allow those relationships to thrive?

Relationships can be confusing and difficult and things that are confusing difficult can produce fear. In this case, fear of someone who is different from you. Fear of someone rejecting you. Fear of not living up to someone's expectation.

In the midst of that fear, we can sometimes feel as though we have no way forward. We can't allow the potential rejection to touch us. We can't allow our own thoughts to be challenged. We can't figure out how to accept the love that others are offering.

All of these fears can keep us from reaching out beyond our comfort zones. They keep us from leaving situations that could be hurting us. They keep us from exploring new relationships with people who will stretch our point of view. These fears stop us from becoming better people than we might be if we chose to allow ourselves to challenge those fears.

As I have confronted the fears that might keep me from some of the relationships in my life, I have discovered that these same relationships have molded me into a much more well-rounded and inclusive person. I have gained a better sense of who I am, and how I relate to the world around me through the process of facing the fears that stood in the way. Rather than looking at how other people might perceive those relationships, I have simply enjoyed the intimacy that I have with the people. As the fear has lessened in these relationships, that has spread to others. I am able to participate more fully in life with a variety of people, thanks to those who are closest to me and the ways that fear has been eliminated.

The authors of the following stories have also had to face fears in various relationships. Andi had to address the fear of loneliness in the midst of an unhealthy relationship with a man. Shanda had to face the fears of her childhood and overcome the fear of returning to a dark depression. Ed had to face the anxiety of becoming a parent and how his own past played into his son's future. Michelle had to battle her own past rejections when approaching the topic of making new friends.

The pages that follow represent some of the most painful examples of fear. But they also represent some of the most rewarding examples of fear being fought and of the authors coming out victorious. As you ponder the relationships in your own life, consider how you can put fear to rest, and begin to experience a more perfect love that casts out fear.

Solitude

Sometimes I sit in my car,

And I just can't move.

I glance at my neighbors' home,

Neighbors whom I love

And I just can't move.

I can't imagine ever moving again.

My car is warm.

And the world outside scares me so.

I am frozen in my solitude.

22

Baby Spiders

By Sarah Moon

When I was seven, I laughed in the face of fear. It wasn't that I wasn't afraid of anything—it's that I thought fear was a silly reason to not do something that I wanted to do. I always won hide-and-seek because I would hide in the dark, creepy basement where seekers were seldom brave enough to look. I only slept with a nightlight so that I could read spooky *Hardy Boys* mysteries late at night by its light. I climbed the tallest trees, and I ate all my vegetables so that I could grow another two inches and ride the roller coasters at Cedar Point.

I wasn't even afraid of spiders. Sure, I knew spiders were scary looking, and that some of them could bite. But I wanted see them up close—I wanted to know if they *really* had eight eyes, and how all those eyes fit on their tiny heads. I wanted to watch them spin their webs and I wanted to watch the egg sacs in the corners of my parent's garage so I could see how small the babies were when they hatched.

My childhood was marked with adventure and curiosity. The world around me was a scary place, but I was more afraid of missing out on life than I was of spiders or the dark. The world was too fascinating to run away from. Fear did not keep me from experiencing the world around me. It was a path to the beauty of those tiny baby spiders.

As I grew up, those baby spiders turned into different curiosities. I wanted to go to college and learn more about life. I wanted to be an astronaut, or a doctor, or a musician, or anything else that would satisfy my thirst for knowledge and beauty. I wanted to travel the world and experience the beauty of it. I had dreams and goals, and I wasn't about to let something as insignificant as fear get in the way.

But when I was seventeen years old, all of that changed. Fear became, not a gateway, but a wall—a wall that kept me from experiencing beauty and from exploring the world. A wall that boxed me in to one way of life and kept me out of the life that I had always hoped for. A wall, towering and colossal, that stood between my dreams and me.

It's amazing and terrifying, the impact that one person can have on your life. It still baffles me how one teenage boy managed to take a girl who was once the world's bravest seven year old and turn her into the world's most frightened seventeen year old. How one teenage boy single-handedly built the massive wall of fear that I'm still tearing apart, brick by brick, today.

I started dating that boy when I was sixteen. I was still ambitious and curious. Fear was still just a gateway to adventure and I was still itching to pass through it. Like most sixteen year olds, my dreams changed from week to week—sometimes I wanted to be a rock star, other times a missionary to a far-off country. But I had dreams and they were bold and courageous. My boyfriend didn't like that.

My dreams awakened his insecurities and reinforced his own walls of fear. Instead of tearing down those walls, he put all of his effort into sharing them with me. When I showed curiosity, he belittled me for my ignorance, convincing me that I was "stupid." When I told him about my dreams, he convinced me that, as a female, I was neither able nor allowed to fill such lofty positions. When I showed independence or initiative, he became angry and controlling. When I excelled at something, he accused me of showing off—he convinced me that my talents were something to downplay and feel guilty about.

I remember him yelling at me for getting better grades than him because I was "making him look bad." He insisted that my good grades were not the result of my intelligence or hard work, but that I got lucky or was a teacher's pet. He ridiculed my college plans, telling me it would be too hard for me, and convinced me that, because I was a woman, all I was good for is marrying him after high school and becoming a housewife. He told me these things, over and over, calling me stupid every chance he got, until I started to believe him.

My dreams began to seem distant and evasive and the world began to seem cold and cruel; I was sufficiently convinced that I wasn't good enough to handle such a big, scary world. When my boyfriend began building walls around me, I didn't object. In fact, I eventually became grateful--he was using fear to protect me from the objects of fear. I forgot the beauty of the world and of those baby spiders. I forgot my dreams.

I learned to be content within the walls that my boyfriend had built around me. My dreams changed--became small and limited. "Safer," he told me. "More realistic." And my new dreams were not my own. Independent thought was not allowed within these walls. Convinced that, as a female, I was too "easily deceived," I trusted my boyfriend to make the decisions, and to protect me from the spider bites of the world. Paralyzed by the fear that he had instilled in me, and feeling devoid of talent and value, I surrendered my dreams to his and tried to be happy. I stopped studying in school and let my grades drop because I was afraid of making him angry if I did better than him. I stopped cultivating my skills in music, afraid that practicing my piano would earn me a session of mocking or yelling. I stopped looking at different colleges or imagining future careers and surrendered myself to a life of serving the man that I was afraid of.

But it's hard to be happy when surrounded by walls of fear--especially when the light from a beautiful, unexplored world keeps shining through the cracks. I ached for that world, deep down, despite my fears. I thought, "*What if* I went after my dreams anyway? *What if* I tried to go to college, even though it's going to be very hard? *What if* I tried to be a missionary or a rock star or an astronaut, even if I'll probably fail?"

I voiced these thoughts to my boyfriend one night, and he got angry with me and grabbed me, and shook me until I felt like my brain was going to splatter against the inside of my skull. So I took off my shoe and threw it at his head. I stood up for myself. I faced the *real* object of my fear. As that worn out, left Chuck Taylor hit my boyfriend bounced off my boyfriend's skull, I felt a brick loosen in the wall of fear that had surrounded me for months. Three months later, I had loosened enough bricks to escape that relationship.

I haven't spoken to that boy in years, but the walls of fear that he built around me are still there. They've been beaten and broken and mostly lay in shambles, but every now and then I come across a segment that still stands tall. Every now and then I still trip and find myself face down in a pile of bricks and wonder if my fears are really worth facing.

Even now, as I sit here, pouring my soul out into my words, fearing the exposure that comes with that, I wonder. I wonder if this fear is worth it to achieve my dream of being a writer. But I look at the corner of the window near my kitchen table and I see a spider web. The light from the sun catches it and it glimmers. I see a baby spider, hard at work, using its tiny legs to create one of the most beautiful and intricate things in the world. I see that baby spider, and I know.

23

Please - Just be My Friend

By Michelle Woodman

Friendships can be tricky balancing acts in my mind. Forget all the flowery quotes about friends being the people who walk in when the rest of the world walks out, or how they are the family you choose. I'm not saying those things are not true nor that I haven't experienced them in my own life. But such sentiments are not applicable to all friends.

There are, for instance, those who will hang out with you until they can be with their "real" friends. Take my elementary school friend Betty*. We had been best friends for two years when, on the first day of fourth grade (and our first day at the new school building) she informed me she would be playing with another friend who was a grade or two ahead of us. She left for the playground without even a backwards glance. I didn't even have a chance to ask if I could at least play with the both of them. No words came, but the hurt did. And I tried to let Betty know by following her around the playground, but she was unmoved by my tear-filled looks. She had her friend, and that was that. I don't recall really talking to anyone about what happened beyond the necessary details. Yes, we were no longer friends, and that was pretty much all I had to say on the matter. I tried to tell Betty how I felt and it didn't help bring about reconciliation so I didn't see the point in talking to anybody else about it. I eventually found some other people to spend recesses and lunch breaks with. Betty's family moved away not too long after that, but it was barely a blip on my radar. And I never did have a desire to get to know Betty's "real" friend.

Then there are those who you are friends with for years until one day, they inform you the friendship is over. The first time that happened to me was in junior high. One minute I thought things were fine between Tanya and I (even though we are not as close as we once were), the next she was bluntly informing me we shouldn't be friends anymore, before continuing down the hallway. The hurt came again, but this time words did not elude me. I had a problem that needed to be fixed, and fast. After all, if Tanya was ready to cut things off in such a fashion, who was to say others within my social circle were not ready to do the same? So I hurried after Tanya and begged her to reconsider her decision. I would change. I would fix whatever unknown wrongs I had committed against her. Just please -- still be my friend.

Tanya said she would think about it.

And she did, deeming me worthy once again of her friendship, but as with Betty, it was never the same after that. How could it be? She was ready to toss me aside, and I willingly gave up a bit of my self-respect to ensure it didn't happen. It's not exactly a good foundation for a relationship.

The hardest sort of friendship, though, is the one where one side has piled too much on the other person. It may not be done intentionally, but it doesn't make it any easier to deal with.

Unknowingly or not, they expect you to somehow fix them, to fill in their gaps and put your seal of approval on them. I was that sort of a friend to Christine. I dumped on her all my negative opinions about myself, all my doubt and insecurities about what my future could hold post-graduation in terms or career and relationships. Somehow I thought this was okay because I was "being real" and "being honest" by sharing my negativity with her. What I failed to see, however, was I rarely listened to her in terms of both her advice and her own struggles. So I took and took, piled and piled my garbage onto her until one day in senior high she gave me a note explaining she couldn't do it anymore and needed to distance her self from me. Again, there was hurt. Words were penned and eventually spoken. And sadness cast its hue over it all because I really didn't want to lose the friendship of someone I had known for so many years. I knew I wasn't always the most fun person to be around with my insecurities and basement-level self-confidence. So for Christine (and for myself) I tried to change. We did what we could to patch things up, yet once again things were never really the same. There was a distance there that easily translated into us losing touch after high school, even though we lived for a while in the same area post-graduation.

With those memories and experiences hiding in the corners of my soul, it seemed only logical after that to keep people at arm's length. After all, I reasoned, if the sharing of the 'not pretty' parts of my life drove people away from me, then it was better for me to tuck that stuff away. I would be upbeat, I would try harder to fit in, and I would keep things on a more superficial level because that is what kept one's friends around.

It was a crappy policy to adopt. I couldn't sustain any long-term friendships with new or old friends, which was the opposite of what I wanted. But I still pressed on, not realizing the lack of emotional investments -- given or received -- in my friends made it easy for us to drift apart at the slightest change in circumstances or geography. I also failed to realize at the time I genuinely was expecting far too much of my friends. I was looking to them to buoy me up, to silence my insecurities, to affirm me, and to give me worth and value. That was (and is) far too much to ask of any human being, never mind kids or teenagers.

When I became a Christian, I would love to be able to say all those doubts and insecurities went away. They didn't. Even as messages about God's grace and big love and vast mercy filled my ears, He was in my mind another someone I had to tiptoe around. Too many missteps, and boom -- He, too, would be ready to wash His hands of me. No, I had to earn His approval, work hard to keep His grace, and not overdraw on His mercy.

Thankfully, God proved me oh-so-wrong in this area. Finally, the reality of His grace and love and mercy is making its way into my heart. This is due in no small part to some very patient people -- who are very good friends -- in my life. My first real "guy friend" (who I later married!) continues to be a great encourager. He reminds me often I do have value and worth because I'm God-designed, because I'm "me". And that being a Christian doesn't mean I have to be (or necessarily will be) perfect on this side of heaven. My sisters are my best female friends, and they're not afraid to call me out on my crap. If I'm getting too wrapped up in myself and my problems, or making a problem bigger than it actually is, they'll tell me to lighten up. They remind me silences between friends are okay, too, and that my house doesn't have to be perfect to have people over (both things I struggle with). We can share our victories, and support one another in our defeats for true friendships involve a mutual give and take. It is this mutual sharing which makes the relationship stronger, and gives each person room to grow.

It's still not all sunshine-and-rainbows, mind you. It's still a scary thing to let God into the messy and empty parts of my heart and soul. However, I am realizing if I let God fill what were God-shaped holes in my life all along, then and only then will I be truly filled and complete. I'm also learning to show more grace to myself and to those around me when we do muck things up. As such, I'm finally growing the type of friendship that was elusive to me in my younger days. I'm learning to press on despite lingering fears of rejection because, with God (Philippians 4:13) I have good friends and I can be a good friend in return, proverbial wards and all.

**Names changed to protect privacy.*

24

The Fear of Being Real

By Jennifer Gage

If everybody is hurting, why is everybody "fine" when you ask? Why aren't we connecting? I have wondered about that my whole life. But I've come to understand why.

In general, we are all told from a young age that no one really wants to know about our hurt. We are told to endure, and press on, and do better, and do more. We are encouraged to find ways to cope and we're discouraged from asking for help. We're told by our families to not admit emotional injury, talk about your problems, or even express sorrow.

The reason we aren't connecting is because we don't want people to know that we can't handle things on our own. We don't want people to know that we need one another.

We work so hard to be self-sufficient, and we don't want anyone to know that bearing all of it, every day, is really too much for one person.

Because, wait for it-- everyone else can do it. It's not too much for everyone else. It's just too much for us. And we do find that we CAN do it alone, but not well, and not all the time.

We were made for community. We fight against our natural inclination because we want to hide the fact that we get overwhelmed and discouraged. We feel isolated. Because the overwhelm and discouragement is not to be spoken of.

We aren't connecting because we don't want people to know that we feel pain, confusion, doubt, loneliness, and despair.

We aren't connecting because we have learned that people don't want the truth. Because truth is messy. Hearing the truth about how someone is really doing requires other people to stop what they are doing and invest into others. We learn early that they are far too busy with their own lives for that. We don't want to burden people with our worries, our insecurities, our pain. We look at sharing those things as a burden to them, because past experience has shown that most people don't care.

Opening up and being real requires too much risk. Risking our pride, risking being thought of as weak, incompetent, or worse. Risking exposure to condemnation, judgment, laughter, and derision. What if you found out that you've opened up to the wrong person because they make you feel worse for being honest? That's devastating.

Risking those reactions while you are in pain is really too much for most of us.

We aren't connecting because we're afraid of being real.

When my third daughter was about 12 weeks old, I reached out to my church for some help. My baby was waking like a typical newborn does, and I also had to get up in the night at least once or twice with my 3 year old, who had always dealt with sleep issues. That was a minimum of 5 times a night.

I think I must have asked for help similar to what you might get right after your baby is born, a few meals, maybe someone to come over and help pull the house together, I don't really remember. But I was informed upon reaching out that my needs did not fit into the comfort and care demographic, or the hospitality demographic, and that there was really not anything they could do to help me. I was essentially told to suck it up, and ask my friends if I really needed anything.

My friends were all homeschooling moms of 2, 3, 4 children too. I had no local family, either. Nobody could actually help me.

And no, that didn't take any courage at all, to approach my church and admit that I couldn't do it on my own. (sarcasm).

And yes, there was a significant amount of shame I felt at having been rejected by my church when I came to them with a burden.

Was I ever real with that church again? No, I wasn't.

I wasn't real with anyone for several years after that experience. I went into survival mode. After being rejected by my church when I asked for help, I had no courage left to ask anyone else.

I had no one with whom I could be real. No one who I wanted to risk trusting with the real me. I had to put on the "everything is perfect" face every time I interacted with people at church or over for dinner or on play dates with friends from church. Nobody else seemed to have such a hard time keeping the house and themselves together, no one else seemed to be unhappy in their marriage, and I just sort of checked out. I locked down and went numb.

I was going to church, to homeschool co-op, I was talking to girlfriends on the phone, I was occasionally getting out for dinner or to go to a movie with a friend, everything looked nice and normal and suburban. No one ever asked how I was doing, and no one ever invited me to be honest about how I felt. I lived in this place where I was totally devoid of emotional interaction. When people asked how I was, I told people what they wanted to hear. Who I was just simply didn't exist anymore. There was only my facade.

I didn't connect with anyone, I didn't have any conversation about anything deep and meaningful. I don't even remember most of that time in my life.. I went to bed every night feeling horrible about myself and my life, and with loads of guilt from the thoughts swirling in my head. Waking up under crushing depression each morning, just surviving and putting one foot in front of the other, and not talking to anyone about how messed up, worthless, scared, alone, and isolated I felt.

About two years ago, when my well-crafted suburban wife and mom facade started to crumble, I faced the fact that I needed to start talking about what was going on inside, and what I was going to do about it.

I had two intense emotional experiences almost back to back that re-introduced me to the person I used to be and that gave me the courage to be that person again, without fear or shame.

The first moment that led to the facade crumbling was the night I had to pull over to the side of the interstate because I was crying so hard that I couldn't see to drive. I had become so callous and withdrawn that I had been unable to do more than tear up and get misty eyed for several years, and the fact that I had to pull over was a shock to me. My heart was broken wide open, and I was crying on behalf of a friend of mine, listening to a song that had great significance to his story. He'd let me all the way inside and trusted me with his darkness, self-hatred, loneliness, and isolation, and I know that he felt that the lyrics to this song were autobiographical. Finding myself, forehead resting on my wrists, sobbing on the side of the road for pain that wasn't even mine was a crystallized moment in time that I may never forget.

That experience was not only important for my sense of compassion and empathy, but because of it. I was able to feel my own pain for the first time in years. I hadn't realized until then that I was in the same place my friend was. I had been so depressed, isolated, lonely, and hopeless that my friend's pain resonated with me to the point of shocking me into wakefulness. It was just that so much rage had been clouding what was really going on inside.

The second moment was actually a combination of experiences that happened at the Blissdom blogging conference in 2010. I had a number of online friends that I was hoping to see, some for the first time. I was completely overwhelmed at the reaction my friends had to seeing me. There was so much genuine happiness and joy coming in my direction that I actually retreated to my hotel room and cried. Again with the tears. I felt like a scar was being ripped open, and I laid on my bed, realizing that there used to be people that reacted to seeing me in that way. There was a time when those reactions were part of my everyday life. And it was because I was being myself. Because I was allowing other people to really know me. These online friends, they knew my heart because of the transparent way I write. And they had made me believe that they really cared about me, not just online, but now in person.

That's when I met Jana. She was the first friend I met after I decided I was going to open my heart up and be who I am again.

We spent 15 hours straight together on the last day of the conference. We attended sessions and whispered and giggled during them like a couple of teenage girls. We sat together at lunch. We skipped a session or two in the afternoon and connected, discussing expectations of others, having to hide who we are and the things we had experienced, over autism and motherhood and love. We walked around the hotel, getting lost and making sarcastic remarks and finishing each other's sentences. We laughed so hard we couldn't breathe.

Over sushi that night, my new friend said something that stunned me. Her words affected me deeply, all the way down inside my soul, where the real me comes from.

She said "I feel like there's nothing I could ever do to make you not love me and accept me."

I had been able to communicate to this new friend, in the space of the first 15 hours we had spent together, that I loved her unconditionally.

That scar that I felt like had been ripped open by feeling accepted for the first time in years? Jana, by speaking honestly and transparently to me, about me, healed that pain. I had spent the weekend feeling open and exposed in a way I hadn't in a long time. But I felt validated, accepted, and most of all, successful, in being who I am. There are no words to express how grateful I am for Jana.

Through those two experiences, and in more of that kind, I realized that when I'm living, interacting, loving from that place down deep inside, I can give my friends confidence in my love and acceptance of them. They know that I care about them; that what they think and how they feel are important to me. That I love them, and I will always accept them for who they are.

When I'm brave and authentically connecting with other people, they are willing to give me the gift of their real self, too. Having the privilege of hearing other people's stories is incredibly humbling. Being trusted with the dark and ugly, with fear and weakness, with insecurity, loneliness, and pain. It's so much richer and deeper than anything I've felt in the last 15 years of my life.

I want that sense of connection and vulnerability and honesty with everyone I consider a friend. I live for that reciprocation, after being without it for so long. I know it's what I was made for. I'm not afraid of being real anymore.

24

Big Fears Come in Small Packages

By David Ozab

"Anyone who makes an offhand comment about her cleft lip gets a punch in the face."

I knew Julia wasn't joking.

"From whichever one of us is closest." I wasn't joking either.

We sat in our van outside the pediatrician's office, our daughter Anna asleep in her car seat. She was four days old and this was her first trip out since we returned home from the hospital.

Since we found out about her cleft—through a routine ultrasound in the twenty-second week of Julia's pregnancy—we'd been afraid. We were first-time parents—a big enough adjustment—but now we had more fears: Would she be able to nurse? How would we handle her being in surgery in a few months? How would we react to the cruel, insensitive, or thoughtless comments?

We told everyone in the family about her cleft lip shortly after the diagnosis, and the picture we chose for the birth announcement didn't hide her lip, though it didn't draw attention to it either. So far, everyone had looked right past it and complimented her beautiful black hair, but so far "everyone" consisted of our family, a few close friends, and hospital staff. Today was the first day strangers would see Anna's cleft without warning. What would they say? Would they shy away?

We sat in the waiting room fearing the worst, but the other parents were too busy with their own kids to pay much attention to ours. We watched the fish swim around the large tank in the middle of the waiting room. We got a few smiles and a "congratulations" or two on the new baby, but no one seemed to notice her lip.

"Anna Ozab."

"Right here," I said.

"I'm Janice, Dr. Sanchez's nurse."

Janice led us back to the scales and laid Anna down: "Seven pounds, two ounces."

"She's lost weight," Julia said. "What's wrong?"

"Nothing that I can see. All babies lose weight in the first week or so."

Janice's response didn't ease our fears.

Dr. Sanchez noted her weight loss too. "I want to keep track of her weight this week, but I'm more concerned about her jaundice."

"Will she need to go back to the hospital?" I asked.

"I hope not. As long as her bilirubin levels aren't too high, I can prescribe home phototherapy."

Dr. Sanchez laid Anna up on the table, listened to her heart and lungs, moved her legs to check her hips, and tested her reflexes.

"OK, Anna, all done."

"How is she?" Julia asked.

"Other than her jaundice, she's in perfect health." She looked at Anna. "Now comes the crummy part."

She handed us a referral form and sent us to the lab to get her blood drawn.

We sat across from the lab, next to the appointment desk. Several people walked past us, including a middle-aged woman with dark, slightly graying hair that stopped to admire Anna.

"What a beautiful baby."

We both thanked her.

"My sister's boy had a cleft, but you'd never know to look at him. Surgeons these days can perform miracles."

We thanked her again.

"What's her name?"

"Anna." Julia answered.

"That's a beautiful name," she replied. "I'll be keeping you all in my prayers."

I'm not sure if God had a hand in it, but that first encounter helped. It's not like the cruel, insensitive, and thoughtless comments might not still come, but we knew now that supportive comments would come as well—from people who'd been through what we were going through.

The blood test came back high, but not high enough to require a return visit to the hospital. Instead, Dr. Sanchez prescribed home phototherapy.

It worked. Her bilirubin levels dropped but so did her weight. By Thursday, Anna had lost almost a pound, down to six pounds, thirteen ounces. She was a toothpick and Dr. Sanchez was concerned. She advised us to rent a stronger pump and make an appointment with a lactation consultant.

I wasn't sure what to expect. I'd read about fanatical breast-feeding advocates—like a militant wing of La Leché League—and I knew the last thing Julia needed was a lecture. As we entered the office, the nurse stood up from her desk introduced herself.

"Hi, I'm Lydia. Dr. Sanchez told me you had some concerns."

"I can't feed my baby. I try and try . . ." Julia stopped to catch her breath. I put my arm around her as we sat down, and helped her regain her composure.

"What am I doing wrong?"

"I doubt you're doing anything wrong. Does she seem to latch OK?"

"It feels like it."

"And she's only got a cleft lip?"

"Yes." Julia looked down at Anna, asleep in her arms. "Her palate's fine and I block the cleft with my thumb to make a tight seal."

"That's good."

"Why isn't it working?"

"I'm not sure. How long until her next feeding?"

"Just a few minutes," I said. "We feed her every couple of hours."

Julia nudged Anna awake. Her eyes opened, her face scrunched up, and she screamed.

"Sorry Anna Banana, but it's time to eat."

Anna latched right away and started nursing.

"Is she always this hungry?" Lydia asked.

"Always."

"With bottles too?"

"Yes." I said.

"How quickly does she finish?"

"It takes awhile. Sometimes she falls asleep first."

"Well she's definitely having trouble with suction."

"Is it something I'm doing wrong?" Julia asked. I heard the guilt in her voice.

"Not that I can see, but I have some suggestions. First, what kind of a pump do you have?"

"We bought a pump but it wasn't working very well," Julia said, "so we're renting one from a medical supply store."

"Good. If anything's going to get your milk flowing that pump will. What kind of nipples are you using?"

"I have no idea," I said.

"Can I see one?"

I handed her a bottle.

She sighed. "That's what I thought. Newborn bottles come with slow-flow nipples. They keep the baby from getting too much milk in her mouth and choking. Anna doesn't have that problem."

"She doesn't?"

"No, she can't get enough milk in her mouth."

"And that's why it takes her so long to bottle-feed?"

"Exactly." She handed the bottle back to me. "You'll want to throw all these out, and buy fast-flows instead. She'll have a much easier time."

Anna had worn herself out and fell asleep.

"Let's buy the new nipples today," Julia said. "I want her to get a decent meal."

I heard the resignation in Julia's voice. Lydia took her hand.

"Please don't blame yourself for this."

"I'm trying not to, but it's hard. Everywhere you turn you hear 'breastfeed your baby, breastfeed your baby.' I know I'm a good mother, but..."

I put my arm around her. Lydia leaned forward.

"A lot of women struggle with breastfeeding, but they still bond with their children and become wonderful mothers."

"I guess so."

"I know so. You wouldn't feel this guilty if you didn't love your daughter so much. That love for her is going to come through in so many ways, and she is going to love you just as much."

So we took her advice and continued to alternate breast and bottle. Julia was back at work and I began my new career as a stay-at-home dad. We took shifts at night, and neither of us slept very well. Anna's weight improved over the next seven weeks, but not as much as we hoped.

"Nine pounds, two ounces." I heard the concern in the Janice's voice as she weighed Anna. At two months, she should weigh more than that.

Dr. Sanchez's voice betrayed concern as well. "Her weight's a bit low for her age. How often are you feeding her?"

"Every two hours," Julia replied.

"What's her breast-bottle ratio, give or take?"

"About three-fourths bottle," I replied.

"We're both bottle-feeding her now." Julia added.

"All formula?"

"Yes," Julia replied. "As much as I'd like to give her breast milk, I can't pump enough to fill a bottle."

"Well, I hate to say this," Dr. Sanchez said, "but it's time to stop nursing."

Julia nodded. I think Dr. Sanchez expected resistance, but all I saw was resignation.

"How much are you feeding her?" Dr. Sanchez asked.

"Three ounces a feeding." I answered.

"That's the other problem. You should be feeding her more."

"How much more?"

"Try five ounces. She may not finish it, but let her drink as much as she wants."

Now fear and guilt gave way to anger. Without knowing it, I had starved my baby. Everything I read about bottle-feeding warned about giving too much food. Overfeed a baby now and risk obesity down the line. Book after book pounded the message into my head: "Don't overfeed!" Not one book warned about underfeeding, none of them even said what sized bottle to give at what age. I was furious.

The rest of the exam went well. Anna met or exceeded all her other developmental milestones.

"Now comes the bad part," Dr. Sanchez said. Anna cooed and gurgled back. She had no idea what was coming.

Dr. Sanchez left and after a few minutes Janice returned.

"I'm sorry, but I have to be the bad guy."

More cooing. Anna loved attention. She wasn't too happy about what came next.

She fussed a bit as the nurse rubbed the alcohol on her left thigh. Then came the first shot and the screams.

It never gets easier watching your child get a shot. Julia cuddled Anna and talked softly to her, as the nurse put a Band-Aid on the wound.

"It's OK. Mommy's here and we're almost done."

"Just one more," Janice rubbed alcohol on Anna's right thigh. Another stick and more screams.

She popped the other Band-Aid on.

"All done."

"You hear that?" Julia asked Anna. "We're done and you're such a brave little girl."

She was far braver than we were. Fortunately, she forgot every bad experience about five minutes afterward. We remembered them all vividly. We worried about her weight, we worried about the surgery, and we still dreaded the first stupid, thoughtless, comment on her cleft.

It hadn't come yet. In two months, we received nothing but support and encouragement. Every day, though, the thought crossed our minds: would today be the day?

The day hadn't come and the day didn't come. Maybe people are more understanding or at least more tactful then we gave them credit for, or maybe God steered us toward what we needed to hear and away from what we didn't.

Our fears about Anna's weight were unfounded too. Once we increased her feedings to five ounces her weight shot up. At her three-month appointment, Dr. Sanchez gave us the good news:

"She is doing great. Up to the thirtieth percentile in weight."

"What does that mean?" I asked.

"Well, ideally height and weight percentiles are about the same. Anna has some catching up to do, but she's moving in the right direction."

"That's my girl," Julia hugged Anna close to her. I could hear the relief in her voice. As hard as it was for Julia to stop breastfeeding, I knew she was far more concerned about Anna's weight.

"Now we can schedule her surgery, " Dr. Sanchez said.

It was time, and we had one more fear to face.

We'd faced our other fears and they turned out to be unfounded. We had the best surgeon and the best hospital in the state. We also had our faith, and a strong little girl who didn't know enough to be afraid. It was time to let go of the things we couldn't control and put our trust in God:

Do not fear, for I am with you, do not be afraid, for I am your God; I will strengthen you, I will help you, I will uphold you with my victorious right hand. Isaiah 41:10 (NRSV)

25

The Little Girl Inside

By Sherry Samuels

I looked in the mirror, deep into my eyes. Deeper than I'd ever looked before. As I looked through the chocolate brown iris and into jet black pupil, like a blinking caution light the question flashed before me – *What are you afraid of?*

If my name were Dorothy and I were traveling down a yellow brick road through the forest on my way to see the *Wizard of Oz* with my little dog Toto and new friends Tin Man & Scarecrow, the answer would be painless.

I'm afraid of wild animals lurking in the woods waiting to make me their dinner. I'm afraid of "…lions and tigers and bears...OH MY!"

Unfortunately, my name is not Dorothy. I don't have a little dog of my own. I do have a friend or two searching for *that thing* that will make them feel complete, but they are not made of tin or straw. And while the idea of a little chitty-chat with a wizard sounds fun, I don't believe visiting the *Wizard of Oz* is in my future.

So, the question remains – *What are you afraid of?*

My answer is not painless. Although only asking the question of myself, I was nothing short of uncomfortable as the pieces of the answer leapt in my brain anxious for attention. Each piece of the puzzle posed as a third grade student waiting to be called on with the answer, "Ooo, ooo! Me! Me!"

And again the question pulses through my mind – *What are you afraid of?*

I'm afraid of the little girl inside of me. Every day I see her. She's been there for years...decades. She's been waiting, hoping someone would notice her sitting there, on the stage of her life, being seen but not heard…just as mom expected.

She's waiting for me – the stronger, wiser version of her – to look in, so she can be all she ever dreamed of being. A dancer, an artist and writer. A sister, daughter and companion. Creative, loving and healed. She wants it all.

As she waits, she thinks about her life…our life. She replays moments in time – feeling my fear – pondering how and why I became afraid of her. She thinks about what she did wrong, where she made mistakes. She wishes there was one opportunity (or 1,000) to paint new pictures, make new decisions.

Sometimes she revisits the Saturday afternoon, sitting in the car with her brother, waiting for mom to come out of the drug store. In spite of her brother's pleas to "JUST SHUT UP!" she sang along to the Whitney Houston song playing on the radio, knowing her voice mimicked her idol. And upon mom's return, she tattled, trusting her brother would be reprimanded. And as the words, "You're no Whitney Houston" echoed through the car, a piece of her spirit wilted.

I'm so ridiculous! Why didn't I just stop singing?

Sometimes she revisits the Christmas when Nana, Uncle C and Aunt A came to their house for dinner. Her mouth watered as she gazed at the kitchen table, covered from end to end with yummy entrees, sides and desserts. She was proud to have been her mom's extra pair of hands and was excited for everyone to try the cake she made on her own. By the end of the evening, she was heartbroken as her aunt and brother took turns making jokes about the belly that, after too much of her beautiful cake, poked out even more than usual.

I'm already so fat! Why did I eat so much?

Sometimes she revisits the Saturday in April when she met that tall, cute guy at the car wash. She remembers how he smiled at her, how they flirted and then how they spent much of that evening on the phone. With every compliment about her beauty or intelligence, came an appeal for her to come to his house. Like it was yesterday, she remembers slipping on her best jeans & t-shirt and sneaking out of the house. On the way to his house he whispered "sweet nothings". At his house, more "sweet nothings". In his room, more "sweet nothings". His body crept in and out, but no "sweet nothings". Tears welled up, but no "sweet nothings". Quietly she laid there, hoping for just one more "sweet nothing". The "sweet nothings" were traded for aggressive words. She walked home, humiliated, still aching for one more "sweet nothing".

I'm so stupid! Why did I listen to those "sweet nothings"?

Sometimes she revisits the night she was getting ready for a night out with friends. She tried on this outfit and that, taking a minute to pose in front of the mirror with each wardrobe change. After picking the right outfit, she moved on to hair and make-up. Just when she felt confident in the package she created for the night, she bounced down the stairs to say bye to her mom. "Are you going to do something with your hair before you leave?" Touching her hair she said, *I did* and left. She spent the rest of the night knowing every random laugh and unknown whisper was because she didn't do her hair.

What's wrong with me! Why can't I make myself look nice?

Everyday, as she waits, the little girl inside me thinks of those and many other faulty decisions and blatant missteps hoping she will be forgiven, that I will give her the opportunity to live and grow with me.

What are you afraid of?

I am afraid of the little girl inside of me. I am afraid I will disappoint her just as others have. I am afraid I will hurt her as others have. I am afraid I am not strong or wise enough to nurture the girl inside as she embraces the woman she was meant to be.

What are you afraid of?

I am afraid of the little girl inside. I am afraid that if I don't stand up and take control, the little girl will grow weary and give up trying to thrive. I am afraid that if I don't fully welcome her space in this, OUR journey, the creative dancing sister…the loving artistic daughter… the healed writing companion…will forever be lost.

26

The Day Fear Came

By Ken Hagerman

I never even heard the knock.

"Hey, Dad! Fear is at the door and wants to know if he can come in and ruin your life."

What?!

It didn't go down that way. No one knew. No one came to the door looking to defecate on my world. No one gave me advanced warning that things would be different from now on. It just happened.

I wasn't without some fear before--I just didn't think about it much. Before I was married, I felt fearless. I played hard, drove fast, and never really considered there could be a bad outcome. I was big and strong and smart and **inexperienced**. Then I got married. **This wasn't the day Fear came**.

The day I got married, I lost a little of my edge. This is not a slight to marriage or my wife, as both have been way better to me than I have earned. I had a responsibility now, this wife. She needed me to be around for the long haul. She needed security. She needed a couple a bucks for a sandwich (or in her case a king-size Snickers and a pint of milk).

I lost a portion of my edge when I had to make room for concern. **Concern is the second-cousin-once-removed of fear**. I realized I couldn't keep acting like a poor-man's Steve O from Jackass. I had to be a little more careful, prudent, wise. Someone was counting on me and I had to act like it.

A few years and a couple of kids later, this got upgraded to Concern 2.0--something akin to worry. **Worry is the mother of Fear and she's a little promiscuous**. This nasty little parasite gets in you and if you're not careful, she gets pregnant and spawns full-blown Fear. There were now two little chunky heads AND their mom depending on Dad. They were expecting me to point this crapshoot called life in the right direction. Pressure, sure. However, **this wasn't the day Fear came.**

In our travels through Paraguay as missionaries we met some really cool volunteer doctors. They offered to give us the once-over. Basically, the ten cent tour of health. Christie and the girls flew through their check-ups like the Blue Angels, but mine screeched to a halt. It was like ticket sales to a Ben Affleck film. **That's when my Worry got frisky with my Stress and conceived a black-hearted little tyrant, Fear.**

Fear didn't kick the front door down like on COPS when Bobby Jo is cooking meth in the back bedroom. It slipped in the side door like the cable guy, here to give you twenty more channels for free. At this point, Fear was dormant, poised for the opportune moment. That day I found out I had a jacked-up aortic valve and that 205 over 40 was bad blood pressure.

A series of tests confirmed I could die. **What?!** I never considered it possible that I would ever die. Now it is not only possible, but without treatment, probable.

BOO! Down with mortality.

My active life was reduced by my physician to "no activity and only one trip on the stairs per day." I am a certified trainer and I loathed the idea of sitting around. After my initial fall from immortality, my anxiety subsided. Having few physical symptoms lulled me into believing I was still Superman. Little did I know my Kryptonite lay in waiting.

The day Fear came was a beautiful sunshiny day, two days prior to my heart surgery. We went to an eco-reserve to rappel and hike on hanging bridges and ride zip lines. **It was adrenaline heaven for a former Invincible**. I needed that day. I was sitting around getting fat on air.

I felt alive again. I completed all of the challenges, even the rappelling. At the bottom I reflected on how wrong the doctors were, seeing that my only symptom so far was muscle weakness due to inactivity. At that very moment, **Fear had just 007-ed his way into my control center** intent on paralyzing my reason.

The adventure was finished; all I had to do was hike back to the park office and leave. It was a little over a mile. Uphill. In the blazing heat of a Paraguayan summer. The inefficient pumping of my damaged heart couldn't keep up with the oxygen demands of my spent muscles.

"Let's start back early in case I need to rest on the way out," I told my wife. I did need to rest, a lot. Our group passed us about 10 minutes into the trek. Thirty minutes later, the group behind ours passed me. I got to the point where **I could only walk about 20 yards then rest for 10 -15 minutes.** I sat on the side of the trail sucking oxygen. I was breathing fine; it just wasn't getting to my muscles. I thought I may die before reaching the top. I did make it out of the woods, albeit more than an hour behind. It was a humiliating affair. The last break I took was just outside the tree line. I was only 30 yards from my cheering friends but I had to sit and pant.

Fear seized this key opportunity during the onslaught to galvanize a place in my head. With its spot carved out, it set about doing an **extreme brain makeover**. It staged several coups while I was in the hospital, each time forging a new room in his fortress. But the worst was some time later, after the surgery and after my release.

I would be punished for eating a bowl of chili too late at night. The roiling gas pains later would wake me with thoughts of a defective replacement valve or a heart attack. Or worse yet, a thrown blood clot. My standard Rolaids moment turned into a life or death assessment. I would lie in bed, eyelids stretched across wide eyes, trying to determine if I should wake Christie. Wake her to tell her goodbye, I love you and risk not dying and looking like an idiot pansy. Or, don't wake her and possibly horrify her with my cold stiff corpse in the morning.

Eventually the pressure would ease and with it my lunacy, only to reappear when I twisted wrong and my incision wound cry foul.

It's been a process for me to reassert the peace of God in my life. There's more to it than just knowing peace is mine, than just reading it in the Bible. I had to put a blade in the gut of Fear and **commit homicide**, then reunite my soul with the Truth, Jesus.

I also had to confess my fear to my wife. Without mustering the nerve to share this embarrassing lapse, I felt frightfully alone. I felt like, as the man of our home, it was my charge to be protector and provider. How could I complete these tasks in such a fragile state? My immortality was dead. How could I regain the stable strength to lead our home?

I have found that since recognizing the very real specter of death, I appreciate life that much more. The contrast has drawn into focus those things that mean the most to me--my wife, my kids. They don't expect me to fly or leap tall buildings. They just want to be by my side come what may.

What I perceived as a loss of my edge turned out to be the key to my victory. The vulnerability to let my wife and kids inside of my private world of dread is what I needed to overcome Fear in the end.

Now, if Fear tries to tickle my terror in the night, I pray with my wife and Jesus sings my soul a lullaby. Peace filters through me and I drift back into His restful arms. It's not foolproof yet, but I'm working on it.

Some say Fear is a survival instinct. If you bow to it you may survive, but the question is will you truly live? I was surviving, but now, with my family and my God, I live.

27

What If We Were Real?

by Kelli Woodford

The salsa is thick.

Cheap tortilla chips hardly do it justice, and it gets pushed all over the plate by his amateur three-year-old fingers.

Because his eyes aren't on the salsa. They're on his Dad.

He scoops like Dad, crunches like Dad, swallows like Dad.

He knows it well: eating salsa and chips is like Dad.

I glance at this rite of passage before my eyes as I cube the potatoes for dinner. At his attempt of manliness. This fellowship over cilantro.

But I am caught by a word, whispered deep, as I watch my double-dippers.

Fragments.

Chips crumble, they stagger at the immensity of the task. To carry black beans, corn, tomatoes, green peppers and onions all safely to into a waiting mouth? For some, it is just too much. And they leave bits and pieces of themselves there, abandoned in the chunky calico abyss.

I think I might be a bit crazy, here, this hot summer afternoon, listening to the hum of the air conditioner as we near 110, but I start to feel it.

Flaky. Like a snappy tortilla chip.

And I know deep down, I have *fragments*, too.

Places I have jumped ship. Towels I have thrown in. Failures and losses.

When impatience rises hot in my voice after the fifth interruption, or the dimpled, chubby fingers of eager toddlers are the last thing I want to see carrying my water glass. When I greet my husband at the door with only a nod, and turn right back to what I was doing because I can't put it down to let him know he matters to me. When the day seems like a battle to be fought -- a war for my own will to be done -- rather than a joy to be surrendered. Yes. These fragments, I have known.

I stagger, too -- *often, even* -- at the immensity of the task.

And this doesn't surprise me. Or God.

But here's the big question, the one that doesn't want to be typed: does it surprise *you?*

Because I guess the thing that I don't want to do with these fragments is let them be known. For me, it's an all-or-nothing kind of world. And if I let *you* see my fragments, my incomplete process, will you think I've abandoned the whole thing? Will you count me among the defectors? Will your love continue when my walk becomes a crawl?

It was that great saint of old, Thomas a Kempis, who wrote it ages ago, *"as a man is within, so he judges what is without."*

And my all-or-nothing? Well, it's a tall order. Both *within* and *without*.

Maybe this is why I prefer to keep it under wraps.

Because it hurts me more than you know. It hurts me more than even I know.

And maybe this is why God has given us His crazy, upside-down but right-side-up Word. **Full of fragments**. To teach us that our all-or-nothing attitude? Well, it's not how He sees things.

I mean, think of the people He blessed in the Scriptures. Jacob was a schemer and a liar. Clever to the point of wondering who was behind his apparent successes (remember that goat breeding thing, in front of the reeds) -- him or God? Wow. Now, there's evidently some mixture there. And Jonah? First he ran away and then clung hard to God after his underwater adventure, finally seeing his need for the mercy of forgiveness. *But then*. Yeah, you know the tale. He whined, pouted, and threw a fit when God was showing that very same mercy to others. Talk about blind-spots.

What do you do with Hezekiah, Asa, Josiah, David, Solomon, and all the other examples in the Kings and Chronicles of men who were *good* . . . but not "to the last drop" ??

(And I'm not even touching Samson.)

This all used to confuse me. It was so inconsistent. So much imperfection. I desperately wanted white to be white and black to be black. Why can't the good guys just *act good* all the time and the bad guys simply *be bad?* There seemed to be so much gray. Such frustrating fragments.

Until.

I looked in the mirror.

Yeah, long and hard.

And I started to see it there, too. Scheming and lying and running and whining. And mercy? Sometimes it's still a foreign language to me.

But no sooner had honesty revealed the fragments, I started to see it. Following close behind, even snapping at the hand that was turning the key in such a dangerous lock. Freeing my shackled wrists from the prison of pride and perfection . . . **it was fear.**

Fear of what *you* would think . . . **if I were real.**

I dump potatoes into boiling water and scrape leftover peels into the garbage. The father-son bonding has continued, and the mess has grown exponentially. The fragments are on the table, on the chairs, and on the floor.

I grab the broom and step into rhythm.

Laughter from the guys and their chips, and while I'm in the same room, I'm not really all there. I'm chewing on this fear thing. I'm unwilling to let go the mess, and just be exposed. And, as my feet dance with my broom, I'm rocked. Like a baby in mama's arms, the motion quiets me.

Then Daddy's voice, like a shaft of virgin sunlight at the pit of a dark dungeon.

"See all these crumbs, here, buddy? All these little fragments? Just scoop them up, too. You can still use them.

Maybe they can't carry as much, but just go in deep . . . ***don't leave all the fragments."***

He sings His lullaby, so sweet, rocking me in these words.

Love dives in deep. Love doesn't leave the fragments. Love scoops them up, binds up wounds, comforts aching scars.

Yes, there's mess involved. Yes, digging deep is costly.

But these things don't turn back Love.

Not inconsistency. Not imperfection. Not mixture or blind-spots.

They don't intimidate God and they don't turn away those who have tasted this Holy Love. The Perfect who gave Himself for all the imperfection.

I see it now -- **We are this to each other**. We can love radically because we have been radically loved.

And as we grow, perhaps the salsa isn't such an overwhelming task. Perhaps we don't break into pieces as easily as we once did.

But part of the mystery of this Love that lives in our hearts is that it *never forgets*. It never despises where it has been and the cracks it now wears.

It has learned a new language: Mercy becomes its mother-tongue.

For this is the secret strength of love. To look at the mess and the salsa-covered fragments . . . and know this is not the end.

It is the *beginning*.

28

Hurtling toward Africa: Adoption and Fear's bluff

By Kim Van Brunt

It happened on the way to Uganda.

My husband, Nathan, and I were finally flying to Africa to meet our son. After months of work, thousands of dollars, and huge stacks of paperwork meant to convince the Ugandan courts and the U.S. government (and maybe ourselves, too) that we were fit for this adventure, we were finally on the plane. We had waited for this day, prayed for it, tried to speed its coming, shed tears in the waiting.

We had known about our son for a short eternity of two months after accepting the referral to adopt him. Being separated from one of your children by an ocean and a continent is disorienting. All my instincts were in overdrive: My heart longed to nurture him, to scoop him up and love him, to wake up with him in the night to feed and care and change. I needed to press my nose into those cheeks. I wanted to comb my fingers through his awesome hair, to look into his almond-shaped eyes, to *know* him. Whenever I stared at his picture or got a new update, my chest physically hurt. He was just too far away. I prayed he was being loved, grieving that I couldn't do it myself yet.

So when the news came that we could fly to Uganda to get him, I was already halfway packed.

The trip to the airport and onto the plane was full of nervous energy, an electric feeling that bounced my knees and raced my heart. I was all adrenaline, pushing ahead like I was fighting through the crowd to get to my son. I didn't understand how everyone in the airport could act so calm when our lives were about to change forever.

After we were finally in the air, the hours began to stretch and the ocean became all we could see. I settled back into the tiny, sagging airplane seat, willing myself to breathe normally. I knew the flight would only feel longer if I kept anticipating, looking for, and longing. I tried to reason with myself that it couldn't be good for my heart to be racing continually.

To take my mind off the moment just hours away, when my son would be borne into my arms, I played a vapid romantic comedy on the seatback in front of me. I was only half-watching while I practiced deep, meditative breathing to keep adrenaline at bay.

It happened during a particularly average scene of the movie: Without warning or reason, the hair on the back of my neck stood up. I began breathing like I'd just finished sprinting across a football field. Except this time, it wasn't nervous energy or excitement.

It was Fear.

Fear with a capital F, huge and suffocating.

I thought of our little family at home, the life we were speeding away from, and I suddenly wanted nothing more than to cancel everything and return to its safety. I knew that I knew: Africa would change me. Our son would change our family. This experience would change our marriage, adoption would change our parenting, and there would be no turning back. Everything we'd wanted, prayed and fought for suddenly seemed crazy. Even dangerous. The fear was both irrational and made perfect, terrifying sense.

Prickling panic climbed up my back and into my neck. My heart pounded in my ears as I silently looked over at Nathan for help, but he couldn't know what was happening in my body. As the stranglehold wrapped around my heart and crept over my face and hot tears began to spill onto my shirt, I had a singular, horrifying thought that seemed one thousand percent true.

We are making a mistake.

It's all wrong, I thought. *I don't want to do this. We have two beautiful children already, a gorgeous home, and a pretty sweet life. What on earth made us sign up for this?*

I closed my eyes. All the months of longing evaporated. I couldn't even see my son's face; it didn't matter. An icy hand was pushing my head under water and I could not breathe. If they can, drowning victims will pull would-be rescuers under the water in a panicked attempt to stay alive. Survival became my obsessive focus.

My next thought was as foreign and frightening as the first.

How do I get out of this?

I could wait until our layover in Amsterdam, where we'd change our tickets and head right back home to our safe, happy, normal, American-dream life. But that was oddly unsatisfying, probably because it made too much good sense. Fear isn't rational.

Instead, an impulse as strong as I've ever felt began to consume my mind: I had to climb over the other passengers and get to the cockpit, to plead with the pilots, to force them to listen to me. The only solution that made sense was to turn this plane around, NOW. I couldn't bear the thought of hurtling toward Africa for one more moment.

Fear was now clouding my vision almost completely as my shallow breaths kept me from wailing. I looked over at Nathan again and felt instant shame. How could I even tell him? He seemed completely fine, watching his own movie, perfectly accepting our trajectory and everything it meant.

By God's grace, what happened next wasn't according to my survival impulses. I didn't clamber over the other passengers. I didn't start scream-crying. I didn't flag down the flight attendant to tell her that I needed to get off the plane. Something inside me, something holy, reached through, whispering *Hold on. I'm here with you, even in this. Reach out. Ask for help.* I stretched my hand across the few inches that felt like miles between my husband and me, finally clenching his arm with a grip that said *please save me.*

He looked over at me, his eyes wide when he saw my face. "I'm... so scared," I whispered in a gritted whimper. "I want to go home. I don't want to do this." My tears were rushing out now. "Please..." I begged. I clung to him hard, trying to escape my terrifying thoughts and the sheer cliff drop-off I was certain was just behind me, threatening to swallow me up.

It must have been obvious to him what was really happening.

"I'll pray for you," he said.

As he whispered the words in my ear and truth washed over me, that small, holy voice inside me began shining its light on Fear, chasing it out. Truth invited grace; grace beckoned mercy; mercy breathed rest. I relaxed my grip. My heart rate slowed as my lungs finally expanded fully with air. The tears stopped. I could breathe again. I could see again.

I swear it was 10 minutes later and it was gone. My son's face floated back into my consciousness and I smiled, nervous, excited. I looked at the Fear that I had just faced, the fear that seemed so powerful it could swallow the entire plane full of people — and it was so small now, so weak and pitiful. Detached from it, I could marvel at the shape it takes from the inside, how it can rush in and replace all other emotion and rational thought.

Over the next weeks and months, Fear would loom large again: Just hours later, in fact, when I held my son for the first time and didn't feel instant connection, Fear was digging its claws into my neck again. When we went into a foreign courtroom, the judge said, "Here's where I have a big problem," and it seemed from all outward appearances that everything was going horribly wrong, Fear nearly suffocated me. After we returned home and I couldn't figure out our family's rhythm anymore and observed helplessly as my other children acted out their own anxieties, Fear whispered to me of my inadequacy and failure.

So it wasn't as if I'd conquered Fear once and for all on that flight. But I can look back at my near-panic attack on the plane to Uganda, on the first leg of the journey that would change my life forever, and laugh.

As large and foreboding and crazy powerful as Fear had seemed in that moment, it was actually showing its greatest weakness. That attack was its last-ditch effort to destroy me, to take me down and push me into living a benign, normal, average life that I was never meant to live. And it picked the eve of the greatest adventure of my life to do it? How obvious. In what it thought would be my undoing, Fear managed only to show me all its cards. It was a coward and a bully. Bluffing is its only credential.

It still makes my heart skip a beat when I think of the Fear that engulfed me while I was trapped in a tiny airplane seat, careening toward a future I couldn't conceive. But I'm so thankful it happened there. I'm relieved it wasn't months earlier when I was filling out that paperwork, because I'm sure Fear catches many in that overwhelming task. Or when we learned more of the uncertainties of international adoption and what it might mean for our hearts and our child's. Or when it was costing more than we'd thought it would. At least at 40,000 feet there was no escape. There was no easy way out.

And now, thanks to those terrible moments on the plane, I have insider knowledge of Fear's tactics and manipulation. I know that when Fear looms largest, there's something worth fighting for just on the other side. I know that Fear makes desperate last-gasps when you're really onto something. I know now that the stronger I feel Fear, the more certain I can be that something amazing is right around the corner.

I found the same truth each time I pushed through to the other side: Fear is just a shadow playing on a wall; an illusion. When it feels the most all-consuming, all I have to do is find my footing, stand up and shine a light. The shadow evaporates, fear looks small and pitiful again, and I'm stronger. And next time, I'll be stronger still.

29

Gobbled Up By Fear

By Mary C. M. Phillips

I had this nightmare that everywhere I looked there was corruption and war and sick people and poverty.

Oh wait. That's not a nightmare.

But things certainly seem dark and surreal in today's world as we move through our busy, fast-paced lives in which time itself is a cherished luxury.

Who can find this intangible treasure? With the daily grind of work and laundry and children and pets and answering emails and returning voicemails and responding to text messages and going to meetings and buying groceries and doing housework and watching little league games and cleaning and cooking and homework and parent-teacher conferences and "Oh, we're out of paper towels" and "Did you put gas in the car?" and "There's no milk in the refrigerator" and…

Time is cropped, stuffed and cramped into the minuscule, when it was meant to be (in its purest form) infinite.

Lack of time produces stress.

And stress then becomes panic.

I remember back in college, suffering from what most people now label as "panic attacks." Waking up each morning, before my foot even hit the floor, they could strike. For no particular reason. Just out of the blue.

While riding the bus one particular day, one blew in like a tornado without warning. No sirens or signals sounded. While wedged between strangers with briefcases and women with babies, BAM! A sudden bolt from nowhere. As it grew in intensity, a girl from my neighborhood appeared next to me and struck up a conversation about a rock band. I couldn't engage. I was drowning. I grasped within a minute or so that she was uneasy with either my tense gaze or sheer lack of enthusiasm in my rather choppy replies. Unable to express my anxiety, she politely moved to an open seat. My burden, my panic, was heavy yet invisible to her.

Nothing had changed. The bus continued to lumber along the usual route. Typical ride. Each road familiar. But as every molecule surrounding me remained intact, an inner tidal wave was in its "backing-up, gaining strength" mode and I was powerless against this levying force; wading in vain on my little surfboard splashing and kicking my way to shore, trembling and puffing, and knowing I didn't stand a chance of making it out alive.

Submerged into the world of "there, but not there."

Many, I'm sure can relate. More and more of my friends are taking prescription medication to keep them from this de-real world of panic. These are good, smart, and talented people. But anxiety rears its ugly into the best of us. It's like a criminal taking away our inner peace and leaving us spiritually destitute. Something is clearly wrong.

I don't think we were designed to live such fast-paced lives where schedules are kept tight and imagination and creativity have no room to scamper about. We tweet, we post, we move too fast. When was the last time you took a leisurely stroll with no set destination?

Peace, although it seems far, distant, and unattainable, is still there though, in the midst of all the chaos. An authentic peace that transcends this foul and often hectic world.

As a seeker, there was a time when every book on relaxation, meditation, and hypnosis filled my bookshelf. Any of the aforementioned may help, but during my darkest time, I needed something more potent.

Potent, yet veiled, having the very nature of peace. Peace itself. Himself. The source. A resilient truth that can stand up against the daily onslaught of media, advertisements, and warnings everywhere I look (even on my food products).

Last week I bought a turkey at the grocery store. It was a 2.34 lb. turkey breast from the deli section's large rotisserie. I buy these turkey breasts weekly since my son is a picky eater (that's an understatement) and will ravenously enjoy them till his heart is content. It's an easy meal. He likes them. Plus, I use the bones to make stock.

What could be stressful about that?

Well, I was told that since the turkey breasts sit under the heating light and are in a plastic-type container, they're unsafe to eat because plastic, when heated, causes cancer. It was the same day I was told caffeine causes osteoporosis. I love my coffee. This news was heartbreaking.

I hear this stuff all the time and maybe there's some truth to it all, but is anything good for us anymore?

I'll be driving along and turn on the radio and will hear the host talking about how I need to fear this person or that person or this party or that party and I get a sickish feeling until I finally switch to another station for a good song.

I'll meet with a friend for lunch and all of sudden am certain they've heard the same program, as they mimic the words that compelled me to turn the radio off just hours before.

Panic and fear are running amuck and I get an earful everyday.

"What if this is the end of the world? Is the government trying to kill me? What if the Chinese fly an atomic droid over the skies of California? Is my food contaminated?" "What if someone is watching me through this computer screen as I write this?"

Uh oh.

What if. What if. What if!

I am so done with "what ifs." Kaput.

Even the little areas that once stirred up fear, have been peacefully crushed since worrying is simply a waste of energy.

I'm not being a careless twit mind you, but I'm tired of being fearful. I'm tired of being in a state of panic. I'm tired of checking every label to see where the item was grown. I'll say a prayer over it and eat it. (I do, however, mostly buy organic items. I'm not an idiot).

I can't worry about Greece becoming a third-world country. They've produced some of the world's greatest minds in the past and it's only a matter of time until another one (with some answers) comes along. God is good and He'll think of something.

In college I carried around Norman Vincent Peale's "The Power of

Positive Thinking" like a Bible. I memorized scripture verses and said them in daily doses like prescription medication. I felt their power; the words I mean. I remember them working in my mind, relaxing my thoughts and directing my focus to Christ who would allow me to do "all things through" Him while he strengthened me. It worked. But I still take a daily dose.

I repeat verses often like a mantra; a salve that absorbs warmly into my flesh and morphs the monsters of the world into tamable, tiny and sometimes even comical creatures.

In the meantime, I'm buying turkey breasts. They are delicious and my son eats them and that's that. (And I buy them early in the day, so they don't sit under those "cancer rays" for too long).

"Do not be anxious about anything, but in everything, by prayer and petition, with thanksgiving, present your requests to God. And the peace of God, which transcends all understanding, will guard your hearts and mind in Christ Jesus." Phil 4:6 NIV

I pray that verse often. It speaks to my heart and allows faith to rise in me rather than fear drown me during the bedlam of everyday life.

Even in the grocery store as I'm buying my son his turkey, I pray that verse. In that scenario, I'm particularly happy when I get to the word "Thanksgiving." I like to think of it as God and me sharing a little pun.

30

Who's Afraid of the Dark?

By Shanda Sargent

"This little light of mine... I'm gonna let it shine.

Let it shine. Let it shine. Let it shine." -Harry Dixon Loes

I'm afraid of the dark.

It's difficult to confess this, because I'm forty-one years old, but I admit it. Darkness rattles me to the core. Since I was a little girl, I've been plagued with this fear. I'm certain this fear has something to do with the fractured home in which I grew up. My alcoholic father hated light, physical light. Even in the middle of a warm sunshiny day, thick heavy drapes were always drawn to prevent even one single shard of light from filtering into our home. The darkness, combined with the stench of stale liquor, hangover vomit, and an explosively angry, time-bomb-ticking father, created a most effective prison of darkness for my little girl self. Our small ranch house was isolated among corn fields and miles and miles of dirt roads. Even at night, no light was allowed into our home. I assure you, you have never known darkness until you have been in the middle of nowhere at night. It was dark, dark, dark.

For a brief time, when I was quite young, I was allowed to have a table nightlight for my room. I can still see the water spill over the top of Niagara Falls as the heat from the light bulb set into motion the inner cylinder of the small lamp. I would gaze at it for hours before falling asleep. That little lamp brought strange peace in the midst of my wrecked home- in the midst of my darkness. It was heart wrenching when my mother removed the lamp from my room. I suppose she thought I was old enough not to need the security of a nightlight. As a result, at the ripe old age of seven, I fell asleep in darkened fear- every single night. I tucked my pink fuzzy blanket securely under my feet and sides. I covered my head leaving only a small slit for air. Even on the sweltering, dead air nights of July and August, I slept drenched in sweat within the security of my pink cocoon. Sometimes, I would carefully prop my knees up under my blanket to make a tent and sing myself to sleep.

"This little light of mine… I'm gonna let it shine."

As I progressed into the teen years, I became a bit braver. Sometimes, my grandfather would work into the night planting, plowing, and harvesting the fields around our house. His presence was security, like my pink cocoon. When he was in the field directly outside my bedroom window, it salved my fear. I would open my window so I could follow the lights of his tractor up and down the rows. The hum of the tractor's motor was comfort. It was then that I would look up at the sky to see God's lights shine. When there was only a mere sliver of a lullaby moon, the stars were the most glorious. I assure you, you have never known starlight until you have been in the middle of nowhere on a clear moon-sliver night. Stars' light beauty in the midst of darkness became a calm, peaceful reminder that the maker of the stars held them in place, and He held me.

When I was nineteen years old, a hero came and swept me away from my house dark. It was a new light-filled beginning. We made our home together, and in each room I found a way to include not one, but two types of nightlights. Hero slept with a pillow over his head to keep out the light, because there was no way I was sleeping in darkness, again. Ever. For our first Christmas, on a budget thin, we purchased electric candles to place in each window. After Christmas passed, the candles remained. To this day, twenty-one Christmases later, we still keep candles in our windows year round. Nightlights and Christmas candles were beacons that guarded against darkness. I wasn't afraid of the dark anymore, because our home was now filled with light.

"Let it shine. Let it shine. Let it shine."

***

Electric light can only chase away physical darkness...

Three years into our marriage, Hero became the senior pastor of a small church. He was also attending school full-time, and teaching a Bible release class at a local elementary school twice a week. My time was taken up teaching third grade at an elementary school that was almost an hour from our home, and running all of the children's ministries at church. At twenty-two years of age, we were both carrying unbelievably heavy loads. In hindsight, it was during this time that groundwork was being firmly laid for a future battle with depression for both of us. We never braked. We chained the load onto our backs and did what we thought needed to be done.

Within the coming years, we were faced with things that were stormy enough to cause the most tenacious person to be jolted. Hero's mother was tragically taken from us in a car accident. Shortly after that, our family was forced, unjustifiably, to leave our church family and a thriving ministry which Hero began two years prior. This "forcing" also left us with no choice but to move across country 1,500 miles to be near the financial and emotional stability of my parents. Almost a year passed, and another long distance move launched us into a tumultuous decade of more church ministry. Still shouldering years of previous brokenness, we pastored a church through a vicious church split, suffered through crushing personal finances, experienced betrayal, hatred, and devastating loss. Somewhere in the middle of it all, Hero stopped vacillating on the teeter totter of depression. He was the first of us to plunge wholly into its steely grip. For years, my hopes and emotions were tossed and jarred on the rollercoaster of his depression. The battle with darkness added weight to the crushing burdens we were already carrying. It was right about the time Hero was able to grasp little snippets of light and claw his way up from the darkness that I plummeted straight down the merciless slope. There was no relief for either of us from the shadows. I was the "strong" one- the one this type of darkness would never touch. When it touched me, I crumbled to pieces. I found myself in the deepest pit I had ever known. I was unable to live, move, breathe. Hero became both father and mother to our four children. He did everything. He carried the church. He carried our family. He cooked, cleaned, did laundry, grocery shopped, schooled our children, and brought me meals into the bedroom I couldn't leave. I was debilitated. Shame swallowed me whole, and chained me to my prison. After one extremely long year of despair, by the grace of God, we were both somehow- miraculously- simultaneously out of the darkness and in the light. Over the years, our battle with depression and spiritual darkness was grisly, unrelenting, and fierce. Now, the little-girl-grown who was afraid of the dark became crippled by the fear of darkness, once again.

I'm afraid of the dark.

I am flat scared that one or both of us will be jerked back into depression's loathsome grip and be devoured. Sometimes, I wonder if worrying about it will be the catalyst that sends me there. What in the world can you do to make yourself not afraid? How can you force yourself not to feel a certain way? Our battles have left us wounded and scarred. We know too well the truth of the despair in the pit. It's hopeless. I don't believe for a second we can pull our own selves up by the bootstraps and make ourselves not afraid.

I've heard it said that fear and faith cannot coexist. Where there is faith, there simply cannot be fear. To those walking in a genuine relationship with Jesus who also experience fear in a very real way, I believe this is a bondage creating lie. If you believe that faith and fear cannot coexist, and you struggle with fear, then your faith will be rattled and shaken. You will question the authenticity of your relationship with Jesus, and you may even question the authenticity of His work in your life. You will begin to doubt God's character and His loving care for you as His beloved child. This constructs a prison of lies that skews your picture of God. The truth is that faith and fear *can* coexist, and *trust* is the bottom line.

Faith is choosing to trust in the midst of fear.

When fear creeps in, you have to wash truth over your situation, and trust that God will care for you. Your trust and dependence on Him is what He desires. I may, indeed, have to watch Hero fall into the pit of darkness, or I may fall into the pit myself. I can hope, and pray, and plead and beg for that not to happen, but if it happens anyway, I have to **trust** that God is holding us just like He is holding the stars. I have to **trust** that He may be accomplishing something deeper that we can't yet see. I have to **trust** that He knows what He is doing, and I am His child. I have to **trust** that in difficult times, He teaches dependence, He grows our faith, and He forges character. Trust. Trust. Trust.

I am still afraid of the dark at times, but I know the One who is the Light. I assure you, you have never known Light, until you have found Him within the deepest darkness. I am His, and He is mine. In Him I lay down my fear in trust, and faith is born. In Him I hope. In Him I believe. In Him I rely. It is Him for whom I sing.

"This little light of mine… I'm gonna let it shine."

"I am the light of the world. Whoever follows me will never walk in darkness, but will have the light of life." (John 8:12 NIV)

Let Him shine. Let Him shine. Let Him shine.

31

Afraid To Love: Afraid To Be Loved

By K D

"Don't allow yourself to make Steve pay for what happened to you in your first marriage," I heard my Pastor say in pre-marital counseling.

"What does that even mean?" I wondered. "Of course I wouldn't do that!"

But the wisdom of these words was tucked away, ready for the day of enlightened understanding. I had been abused in my first marriage. From the first night of my honeymoon, I wasn't good enough. And a week didn't go by before I was called things I had never been called before. I'll never forget the day, just weeks into my marriage when a letter was returned "not deliverable" to our tiny apartment. It was scented with my husband's cologne and written in his hand to an out of state co-worker. I opened it, hands trembling for the ominous shadow that fell over my shoulder and onto the envelope. "I've made a huge mistake," he wrote, "I am in love with you, but I just didn't know how to stop the wedding. What should we do?" His careful script went blurry. I knew this woman, had befriended her on the phone. She was fifteen years older than my husband, and married. The day turned dark, and no amount of sunshine seemed to dispel the darkness.

Hours later, when he came home from work, I confronted him about it. "How dare you open my mail?" He bellowed.

"It isn't your mail *from* someone," I answered, "It was your mail *to* someone!" In answer to this, I was slapped in the face. Hard.

I was unprepared for this type of treatment. I had never seen anyone treated this way. Ever. As a doted-on only-child from a strong Christian family, I had met him at church. He was charming, good looking, talented and had a bright future. He was also the only other person remotely close to my age in the whole church. Never did I see this coming. In our four years of intermittent dating, never had he laid a hand on me in anger.

At some point, a tearful apology was given for the slap and letter. He called it temporary insanity and cold feet, and I naively thought that this made everything better. We are supposed to forgive, right? And it was better, for a while, until he got angry again. Things would go well for a time, but without my noticing, they gradually became worse. Each time he got angry and physically abusive, the beatings were more severe. I was even picked up by my hair several times, and once had an iron thrown at me. The vicious cycle continued on for eight and a half long years. I never told anyone. I was too afraid of him to tell anyone.

In the end, not only did I discover that my husband had participated in affairs with several women, but that he was involved in a Ponzi scheme and would be going to federal prison. I was left alone to raise our three year old son.

After a long and drawn out divorce, an old family friend and widower came to be interested in me. He was kind, gentle and loving in every way. I thought that I'd died and gone to heaven. He had been a close friend with both me and my ex-husband, even visiting him in jail, exhibiting the kind of friendship and love that never fails. Suddenly, I was terrified. What if the problems from my first marriage were all me? What if I brought on the malice my first husband showed me? What if my second marriage proved to be just as painful as the first? What if I turned this godly Christian man into a monster? What if it was all my fault, like my first husband said? What if I couldn't love Steve's children as much as I loved my own? But worse yet, what if all of my patience and forgiveness had been used up, and now when I had a godly spouse, I wouldn't be able to give him the kind of wife he deserved? What if? What if? What if?

There have been days: days of suspicion, days of testing. I didn't consciously try to provoke Steve, but subconsciously I wondered just how mouthy I could get. Would he hit me if I said something really cutting? Of course he didn't, but I caught myself trying to push him to the limit many times. Afraid to love, but even more afraid to be loved.

But I am so glad that I pushed past my fear, and even still more glad that Steve loved me through it all. "Perfect love casts away fear," and he has endeavored to love me the way Jesus loves His Bride, the Church, seeing me spotless and without fault or defect.

Those words my Pastor spoke to me so long ago proved to be such valuable advice. I was so certain that I had come through my past without any lasting scars, but I was far more damaged than I had ever dreamed. And I wondered. What kind of wounds had my first husband encountered to have treated me and others the way he did? Looking back on my past, I realize that hurting people hurt people. My silence not only hurt me, but ultimately hurt my ex-husband, ensuring that there would never be place for healing or reconciliation. But His Grace was bigger than my silence. I only know that God delivered me from a violent man, and placed my son and me in a safe place where we no longer had to be afraid to love or to be loved.

32

Dropping Fear

By Ed Cyzewski

When I found out that we're expecting a child, I started carrying a ten pound weight up and down the steps. Sometimes I did it in my socks. Other times I wore sandals. Sometimes I held my hands out so that I couldn't see the steps. Other times I leaned back a bit on the railing.

This was not a practical exercise per se. This was my way of dealing with anxiety: a sleep depriving fear that I would fall down the steps while carrying our newborn baby. I am a walking worst case scenario survival book. Welcome to my world where terrible things are not only possible but bound to happen.

Since finding out my wife is pregnant, I've imagined all of the ways that I could drop a baby, fall while carrying a baby, or choke a baby. My brain just goes there. It's not like I sit around in the afternoon or lie in bed trying to think of awesome stuff and that's the best I can do. Those images pop into my mind and then the obsessing and fretting begins.

I knew this would be a problem. I just never imagined how bad it would be.

One of the first times I confronted anxiety as an actual problem, rather than something that's just a natural part of life, I was sitting on a dock with members of my wife's family. Her cousin's toddler repeatedly charged toward the edge of the dock, and I quietly freaked out inside. Each time her cousin grabbed the child, turned him around, and sent him back to land until he decided to charge again.

It drove me insane. I had to close my eyes and act like I was taking a nap. In reality, my heart was pounding. In my mind, I could see EMT's fishing the child out of the lake to try to revive him.

Walking back to our cabin that afternoon, I realized I had a problem. No one else was freaking out. What was wrong with me? How would I ever survive having kids of my own? Anxiety like mine wouldn't just turn me into a helicopter parent. We're talking about inserting a GPS chip into the child or tracking him with a spy satellite and encasing him in bubble wrap.

When my family began praying for me that afternoon, I remembered a Caedman's Call song that talks about this world making us drunk on a spirit of fear. As I thought of that spirit of fear, I recalled the verse in Second Timothy that says, "God has not given us a spirit of fear" (2 Timothy 1:7, ESV). Along similar lines, Haggai assured the Israelites that God's Spirit remained among them, so they should not fear (Haggai 2:5).

If God doesn't give us the spirit of fear, crushing anxiety certainly has nothing to do with God. In fact, fear runs completely counter to God's plans for our world.

In that moment I had a vision of sorts. I saw the world restored under God's Kingdom. It was like I'd popped my head down a rabbit hole and found something wonderful and completely different. The world was completely at peace, restored and free from fear.

God gave me a glimpse of a life without fear.

By the time I was practicing "walking down the steps," I'd drifted far from that reality of God's presence. I was lying in bed each evening, struggling to fall asleep while my mind raced with various tragedies and disasters.

I thought I'd been delivered from fear when I received that prayer from my family, but as it turns out, some demons are tough to fight. They only relent when driven out by intense prayer and fasting.

I don't know what exactly is behind fear in my life. If I had to guess, it's a mix of my own fallen nature and a spiritual struggle. When I say spiritual, I mean that there actually are spirits working against us. How can I not think that if the Bible defines the narrative of my life? Paul spoke of a "spirit of fear." The day I started treating my fear as a spiritual force that Jesus needed to combat, I finally started to make progress.

As I faced fear yet again in bed each night and on my way down the steps each morning, I could have despaired that prayer had failed me that day in the cabin. Perhaps I could have popped a few pills to settle my mind. Then again, I could have just given up on sleep. Rather, I tried to remember that I was dealing with a spirit of fear, a spirit who, at least in my case, would only relent in the face of targeted spiritual warfare—namely prayer.

The best thing for me in the midst of my fear and anxiety over fatherhood has been my small group. We have three other fathers with five kids between them. I've gone to them for prayer time and time again. God has used them to help me fend off the spirit of fear.

They've shared their own stories of anxiety before the births of their children. They've told me about the joys of fatherhood. When they pray, it's like heaven is torn open and the Holy Spirit is injected into my brain and lungs. They share with me visions of peace and joy where I'm walking with my son hand in hand. They proclaim that God will carry me, even when all I can think about is falling.

I'm not anxiety-free yet. However, something has broken. The spirit of fear, my own fallen brain, or whatever else has been overpowered and overshadowed by God.

Sometimes we clutch to anxiety like a newborn baby that we assume must be part of ourselves. We believe the lie that letting go of anxiety will make us irresponsible.

Clinging to anxiety will knock us down the steps every time. Letting ourselves fall into God's sustaining embrace is the only way we'll stand.

33

There Are Worse Things than Being Alone

By Andi Cumbo

June

All the flirting. All the giving. All the kissing. It is just like what I have been looking for – HE was just what I'd been looking for.

It has been more than three years since my husband left on that afternoon where I'd had lain sick with fever watching *Must Love Dogs* and wishing my marriage was more like that. Three years of crying and dating when I had no business doing so. Three years of working 60-hour weeks and starting a blog. Three years of friendship and loneliness. Three years of healing.

Now, here I am – single, healthy, ready to try again. And here he is – the try.

We flirt online and then via text. He chats with me on my lunch breaks from jury duty and talks about his favorite movie *Anchorman* (maybe that should have been a clue?). He calls when he says he will, and when I get on a plane to see my brother in Texas, he says he is going to miss me, even though we haven't even met. I am smitten.

So when he suggests that he come to my house on the day I return from Texas, I don't hesitate. That sounds great, I say. And it does.

***

Now, I look back and think, "Wow, he was too eager. I should have known. I should have realized when he showed up and his face was puffy and he'd backed into the toll both. I should have seen that his teasing about my bad directions was the first step toward the blame I would carry. I should have known."

But I didn't.

***

I fall in love with this kind, caring man who wants me as his. It happens on our second date when he does three crucial things:

1. He helps me buy a brand new laptop (the very one on which I now type, in fact) for a good price at a reputable store. Heis willing to share his IT expertise without making me feel stupid.

2. He takes me to meet his dad and asks how he should introduce me. "As my girlfriend?" I'm a sucker for a well-delivered, romantic query.

3. He tells me about a very personal injury that someone in his family had committed against him. Open up your heart to me, and I'll give you mine.

By date three, I am completely gone. Committed, taken, all in.

***

September

I'm sitting at Dunkin' Donuts just down the road from my house. He was supposed to have picked me up before the prospective buyers came to see the place, but he is late. . . so I just walk. No big deal, I say to myself.

Then, he isn't there in an hour. He isn't answering his cell. Or his house phone. Or his texts. Or his email.

Two hours later, the window for the visit is gone, and I am in tears. I give him one last call as I start to walk home, and this time he answers. He had overslept. He is coming.

"I need to be able to count on you," I say. "If you can't be here for me, then I can't do this." I mean it, sort of.

He pulls up two hours later, having driven from home 100 miles away. Contrite. Tired. He can't believe I forgive him. He can't believe I didn't yell. He can't believe I'm not his ex-wife.

I'm not. We walk through Philadelphia. He is tired and sick . . . hung-over maybe, but here. Here with me. That's what I think matters.

***

New Year's Eve

He and my roommate go to the liquor store across the street and buy some tequila, ostensibly for me because I love tequila. He passes out in the recliner at 10:30. I begin to anger.

***

January

There is a massive snowstorm headed our way, so I drive south to his house so we can be snowed in together. I arrive to find him passed out on the couch. I rouse him by shaking him until his head snaps, and he just passes out again.

I go to my car and call his pastor, the only man I know who knows about his drinking. He points me to another man – let's call him Jesse – who tells me that my man has a drinking problem, that he has had several car accidents. Jesse is his sponsor, or was until my man quit trying.

"You have a decision to make, Andi."

I weep in the car outside his house. Then, I go back in.

***

February

He breaks up with me via email. I am angry, hurt, devastated. . . but somehow this seems best, despite the pain.

We continue to talk though. I meet him halfway between our houses, and we take a walk. I cry as he gets ready to leave.

He comes to my house, and we walk and talk. He tells me he wants me to lose 20 pounds. I get angry and then feel guilty. He's right, I think. He's so right.

I tell him I can't see him anymore – that he can't tell me he loves me – especially via text message – if we aren't going to be together. He says I'm right. He continues to text.

Then, the texts stop. I'm beginning to heal. I spend time with friends. I start eating again (15 lost pounds later). He and I talk like friends as he gets himself straightened out, as he puts it.

I come home to Virginia and fantasize about marrying Ellis Paul, the singer-songwriter I get to interview. I have a great weekend with my parents.

On the way back up north, I'm driving past his house and call to say I have his parking pass. Does he want me to drop it by?

"Another time."

I feel the world drop out from under me. "Is there someone there with you?"

I tell him if I can't see him right then, I won't ever be able to see him again. He caves.

We sit in my car and talk. I tell him I wanted him to fight for me. He almost hyperventilates at those words. He goes back to her in his house.

I lose all control. I stop eating again. I cry all the time. I watch countless hours of *Firefly*. He calls and tells me she is an alcoholic. He tells me he misses me but can't do that to her. The drama and damage continue. I hope for him to return.

***

April

My friend calls. I tell her I just want to marry someone. I'm so afraid of being alone, so tired of being lonely.

"Married people get lonely, too, Andi." I can't hear her.

***

May

He breaks it off with her after I show up after having visited his dad on the pretense that his dad has cancer. I manipulate the situation, and I find out that she is really crazy . . . but then so am I.

He calls me one night to say she has cut herself and he doesn't know what to do. It's 1am, the night of the *Lost* finale. My roommate helps by calling the other woman's sister, but my roommate is so angry with me that I can feel her rage through the air, like a radiator burning my skin even as I lean against it to get warm. I drive to him anyway.

We recommence dating, and this time, he's drunk most of the time. I come over most days to find him passed out and sometimes wet with his own urine. He shows up at my house in the middle of the night pounding on the door; he's drunk, and I have no idea how he even made it there.

One day he's passed out at my place, and a man appears in my backyard. I think he's the electrician, who has somehow gotten into our townhouse courtyard, and open the door to realize at that moment that he's a junky and has jumped from the room of the warehouse behind our house. My man sleeps on upstairs. I take him through the kitchen where he tries to hand me a wad full of dollar bills. Past our furniture and my roommate's flat screen TV and out the front door. After the man leaves, I nearly pass out with my own stupidity . . . and then the anger rages through me. How could he not know I needed him?

***

I'd like to think I started to wake up then. But I didn't. Not for months.

***

September

My mom gets sick, gallbladder cancer, perhaps metastasized from the melanoma that she's beaten three times. I somehow know – through the massive insanity that is my life with an alcoholic – that she is dying.

My lease ends, and I move in with him. I come home most days to find him unconscious on the couch. I can't imagine how he keeps a job at a massive government agency. I go to Al-Anon once. It doesn't help, except that it does. Maybe. Now.

I come home one day unable to find my white cat Emily. He has left the back door open, and his littlest cat George has run away again. George can handle it, although I worry. But Emily, Emily's not a suburban cat. I scour the house looking for her, and when I find her under his dress pants in the closet, I collapse into a ball of relief.

And I wail.

I want to die.

***

November

He and I go to my parents' house. My mom is in the hospital, unable to get herself to the bathroom. He stays back at my parents' to help the satellite TV man install a jack upstairs where Mom can watch. When he comes to the hospital, he tells me how hard the visit is for him.

I know. His mother died of cancer ten years before.

I call my brother. Tell him to start making plans to come home. Dad tells me to go home. He'll call every day. Then, we leave and go back north. I teach somehow.

My birthday is that week, Thursday. I come home from class to find him halfway to unconscious. My birthday. The day before I will go home to be with my family as my mother dies.

I call my friends. They offer for me to come. I tell them, "No. I have to go south tomorrow and you're north." His dad comes over after I call, sobbing, to tell him we won't all be going to dinner that night. As his dad sits with me on the couch, my man asks if I want to go out.

I want to scream, "No, I don't want to go out with you when you're half-drunk on my birthday and my mother is dying. No, I don't want to do that."

Instead, I watch NCIS after his dad leaves. He drinks.

The next day I go home.

My mother dies 12 days later.

***

November 25

On the day, Mom died, Thanksgiving Day, I can't reach him. He isn't answering at all. I need him to know. So I call his sisters. They find him for me.

He arrives at mid-day, mostly intoxicated. I am so spent I have nothing to do but be angry, so, so angry. Finally.

We walk out through the yard, and I tell him I'm not moving back. I need time. I need him to get his shit together. That I'm not breaking up with him, but that I wouldn't see him until he was sober. My cowardice begins to creep back in. I put my hand on his face to comfort him.

"I drove all this way for nothing, then?"

He leaves that night.

***

December

I keep trying – a Christmas party with his friends and family, where he asks me what is wrong twenty times. "You just don't seem like yourself." A few phone calls.

But I am too tired.

A few weeks later, just after Christmas, when the letter arrives that tells me he wants to marry me, that if I don't come back he doesn't know what all this pain has been for, I just put the pieces of paper in my Bible and leave them there. Until I ripped them to a million shards and throw them in the furnace.

***

Being alone, well, that isn't so scary now. . . not as scary as living my life every day afraid that the man I love will be dead on the couch when I get home. Not as scary as not being with my mother on that last day. Not as scary as wailing in a closet at the sight of my cat. Not as scary as that.

About The Authors

Preface: Jonathan Brink is Senior Editor and Publisher at Civitas Press. He is learning daily what is means to live into the footsteps of Jesus. He is the author of *Discovering the God Imagination, Reconstructing A Whole New Christianity* (Civitas, 2010). He blogs regularly at jonathanbrink.com.

Introductions: Alise Wright is married to her best friend Jason and is the mom to four incredible kids. She is the editor of and contributor to *Not Afraid, Stories of Living with Depression.* She loves writing, knitting, playing keyboards in a cover band, and eating soup. She writes about faith, family and friendship regularly at her blog, alisewrite.com.

Fear and Your Profession

Chapter 1: Melody Harrison Hanson is a writer of poetry and essays, a fine art photographer and blogger living in Madison, WI with her husband and four kids. She can be found studying Biblical texts, sitting in the sunshine with coffee or a good book, taking endless photographs or writing. Melody was a contributor to Not Alone, Civitas Press, 2011 and Finding Church, Civitas Press, 2012.She is working on a collection of poetry titled: *Going Quietly Sane* and blogs at: www.logicandimagination.wordpress.com.

Chapter 2: Kathy Escobar co-pastors The Refuge, an eclectic faith community dedicated to those on the margins of life and faith in North Denver. A speaker, spiritual director, group facilitator and advocate, Kathy is passionate about community, equality, justice, and change in the church. She has written several books, including *Down We Go: Living into the Wild Ways of Jesus*, *Come with Me: An Invitation to Break Through the Walls Between You and God*, and *Refresh: Sharing Stories, Building Faith*. She has a Masters degree in Management and Organizational Development and a certificate in Evangelical Spiritual Guidance from Denver Seminary and blogs regularly about life and faith at www.kathyescobar.com. Kathy lives in Arvada, Colorado with her husband and 5 children.

Chapter 3: Joy Wilson is the author of *Uncensored Prayer: The Spiritual Practice of Wrestling With God* (Civitas Press, 2011). She and her husband, Bud, are two life-long hippies. They live in Bartlett, TN, with six cats, two dogs, and a timber wolf hybrid. Joy is an Outlaw Preacher and an active participant in Kairos Prison Ministry. You can usually find her at home writing or intently reading history and mystery books. Contact Joy at joyleewilson@gmail.com.

Chapter 4: Rich Chaffins is a worship director, luthier, guitar teacher, and band leader, yet does not find his life one-dimensional. He lives in the 304 with his amazing wife Misty, and their two sons, Nicholas and Wesley.

Chapter 5: Janet Oberholtzer is an author, runner and speaker. An additional bonus due to an active running schedule is that it allows Janet to enjoy more of some other pleasures in life… good food, dark chocolate and fine wine. Janet shares her story of **doing what she can, with what she has, where she is** through writing and speaking. Her first book, *Because I Can* was released in 2011. It is a body, mind and spirit memoir about her recovery and her renewal after being severely injured in an accident. The deadline for this piece was a few weeks before Janet did the full marathon. You can find out how it went at her website, janetober.com.

Chapter 6: Kerry Whalen is a contributor.

Chapter 7: Richard DiPippo is the author of a blog titled *Confessions of A Heretic Husband.* He lives in Newmarket, NH with his wife, two daughters, aged four and one, and a cat. He loves to write novels and computer games.

Chapter 8: By the grace of God, Diana Trautwein has managed to live a lot of interesting lives. While a student at UCLA, she married at 20. Two months after graduation, she traveled to Africa by freighter, brought home a baby 2 years later, had 2 more and stayed home to raise them for 20 years. A whole new career in ministry began in her 50's. Now in training to become a certified Spiritual Director and trying to find ways to write her story down, she continues to look for that last word of love as she meets with seekers-after-God one-on-one, and as she enjoys her 8 grandchildren, ages 2 to 21.

Chapter 9: Addie Zierman is a writer, mom and Diet Coke enthusiast. She's been rejected a lot. But she's also been published in journals like *Defunct!* and *Literary Bohemian* and on *Relevant Magazine* online. She blogs at http://addiezierman.com reimagining faith, one tired cliché at a time.

Chapter 10: Tamara Lunardo blogs about life and faith at TamaraOutLoud.com, occasionally with adult language, frequently with attempted humor, and hopefully with God's blessing. A part-time freelance editor and writer and full-time mom, she holds a BA in English. She almost never holds her tongue.

Chatper 11: Sonny Lemmons spends what he laughably calls his free time blogging at LookThrough.Net, sharing his thoughts on faith and fatherhood. He left a 13-year career in Higher Education

Administration to become a full-time stay at home dad (to Kai, 3) and husband (to Ashley, perfect), which he claims are the best jobs he's ever had. Sonny was a contributing author to *The Myth of Mr. Mom* (Portmanteau Press, 2011).

Fear and Your Faith

Chapter 12: See Chapter 1 for Melody Harrison Hanson

Chapter 13: Aletheia (uh-lay-thee-uh, Greek for TRUTH) Schmidt finds her days full of her favorites—art, reading and writing, and live life with college students. She sits on her floor as much as possible, single-handedly supports good earth tea, and adores hole-in-the-wall-dives. Aletheia is in love with the God who redeems all life and calms all fears, and is always on the hunt to see this good God in all things. For more Aletheia: http://www.accordingtoaletheia.com.

Chapter 14: Sarah Bost-Askins is a freelance writer, poet, and sometimes blogger. She writes for her personal blog *From Tolstoy to Tinkerbell* and co-founded *The Dark Jane Austen Book Club*. She lives in Chatham county North Carolina with her husband Mark, her two stepchildren, and three Springer Spaniels. During her free time, she is a wannabe gourmet, avid reader, and collector of too many books.

Chapter 15: Alicia is the author of this essay and more graduate papers on the art of counseling from a Christian worldview than she would care to count. She is passionate about using her experiences in life to help others overcome the pain of living in a fallen world. Alicia lives in Denver, CO with her husband and their two spoiled black labs. She enjoys cooking, gardening, and anything that allows her to be outside enjoying the amazingly beautiful Rocky Mountains that surround her.

Chapter 16: Travis Mamone is the co-host of the weekly podcast Something Beautiful. He has written for such publications as *Provoketive Magazine*, *Relevant Magazine*, *Burnside Writers Collective*, and *The Upper Room*. He has also contributed to the books *Not Alone: Stories of Living with Depression* (Civitas Press, 2011) and *Finding Church* (Civitas Press, 2012). He lives in Easton, MD, and blogs at http://www.travismamone.net.

Chapter 17: Misty Chaffins is a married, stay-at-home mom to two boys. Living life in small town WV, she shares some of it with readers on her blog at thechaffins.blogspot.com. You can usually find her being a chauffer for the children. Her hobbies include reading, making soap and generally pretending to be creative.

Chapter 18: Jen Rose is a writer, radio nerd, music lover, and hopeless literature addict from small town Florida. She fancies herself a music journalist and poet and has been blogging since she begged an Internet acquaintance for a LiveJournal invite in 2002. Besides writing, she enjoys vinyl records, good coffee, and getting lost in real bookstores. Her Internet home is jenwritesstuff.com.

Chapter 19: Juan M. Guerra was a contributing writer for *Bunnies & Traps: Short Stories - Second Impression* titled "The Dark Labyrinth" in 2007 with actress Brie Larson (Showtime's *United States of Tara*). He lives in Redwood City, CA, and is working on a feature film with director John Fasano (writer of *Alien 3*, *Darkness Falls*) and actress Leslie Eastebrook (*Police Academy*, TV's *Laverne & Shirley*). He is an avid reader and writer, graphic designer, moviegoer, expressive photographer and a fitness buff.

Chapter 20: Daryl Thomson is a contributor

Chapter 21: Lore Ferguson is a designer and writer living in the Dallas area. She has been blogging at Sayable (http://sayable.net) since 2001 and is a graphic designer by day for a non-profit working to rescue and rehabilitate trafficked victims in Mumbai, India. She tweets at @loreferguson. If you meet her expect a hug—it's the only thing she does *really* well.

Fear and Your Relationships

Chapter 22: Sarah Moon blogs at SarahOverTheMoon.com. She is a student at Oakland University, working toward a degree in Women's Studies. Her dream is to become a professional writer (though, astronaut certainly isn't out of the question yet). She enjoys horror novels and deep discussions about whether or not the eagles could have flown Frodo and the ring to Mordor.

Chapter 23: Michelle Woodman blogs at *This Time Around* (http://www.michellewoodman.com), and is the author of seven National Novel Writing Month manuscripts, several fan fiction stories she will share if you ask nicely, and is at work on a proper novel involving spies and coffee houses. She lives southern Alberta, Canada with her husband, their cat and some constantly hungry fish.

Chapter 23: Jennifer lives in Raleigh, North Carolina and works as a freelance writer and social media consultant. She has four children, and enjoys reading, writing, travel, and music.

Chapter 24: David Ozab is currently editing and revising his first book, *A Smile for Anna,* which tells the story of his daughter's cleft diagnosis and surgery, her speech delay, and her incredible spirit through it all. His writing has appeared in *Chicken Soup for the Soul*, *Catholic Digest*, and *Errant Parent*. He lives in Eugene, Oregon with his wife and daughter.

Chapter 25: Sherry Samuels is a blogger (Dancing in the Rainbow) and contributing author for *The Well Written Woman* website. By day Sherry works for a non-profit organization, helping families who have a child with a chronic/terminal illness and by night she works on her book of short stories. A native Midwesterner, Sherry has spent the last 13 years becoming a southerner.

Chapter 26: Ken is also known as The Barba, a blogger who finds therapeutic relief posting about his adventures as a cross-cultural missionary and recovering religion addict at ramblingbarba.com. Ken lives in Paraguay, South America with his fearless wife and two daughters. He loves to stalk blogs, catch fish, and eat small animals seared over a fire near his hammock.

Chapter 27: A recovering perfectionist, Kelli Woodford seeks to live like she prays -- eyes wide open to the beauty in the mess. She credits motherhood and the school of hard knocks with any progress she has made toward this end. Married to her best friend, and mother to seven love-children, Kelli revels in engaging conversation, losing herself in creation's song, and anything peppermint.

Chapter 28: Kim Van Brunt is a professional writer who just recently overcame another fear: Submitting an essay for publication. Kim lives in Rochester, Minn., with her husband and three kids. When she's not writing, she's mothering, practicing yoga, cooking, or doing a combination of all three. She writes about adoption, faith and family at www.kimvanbrunt.com.

Chapter 29: Mary C. M. Phillips is a writer of narrative essays and short stories. Her work can be read in several national bestselling anthologies. As a musician, she has toured nationally for various alternative rock groups and musical comedy artists. Mary lives in New York, drinks too much coffee, and enjoys hanging out with her family.

Chapter 30: Shanda Sargent belongs to her beloved, Matt, and homeschools their four crazy-amazing kids near the foothills of the Rockies. After leaving 20 years of professional ministry, their family recently moved across country and is "ruthlessly trusting" God in the midst of plan B. Shanda blogs at theupsidedownpastorswife.blogspot.com, where she transparently shares her heart's ramblings about life and grace.

Chapter 31: KD is a contributor.

Chapter 32: Ed Cyzewski is a freelance writer who blogs at www.inamirrordimly.com. He is the co-author of *Hazardous: Committing to the Cost of Following Jesus* and the author of *Coffeehouse Theology: Reflecting on God in Everyday Life*. Ed obsesses over hockey and gardens in Columbus, OH where he and his family hang out in the evenings with their house rabbits.

Chapter 33: Andi Cumbo is a writer, editor, and writing teacher whose work has appeared in *Santa Monica Review, PRISM, South Loop Review,* and other publications. She blogs daily at andilit.com, and she and her three cats are in the process of buying a farm in the mountains of Virginia.

About Civitas Press

Civitas Press is a boutique publishing firm specializing in inspiring and redemptive ideas. We specialize in a new and unique publishing model by partnering with inspiring writers who want to develop their voice, create a compelling presentation, and get the word out. We are creating a close-knit family network of writers that are working together to help each other develop a powerful platform.

Civitas Press can be found online at http://civitaspress.com

Twitter: civitaspress

Facebook: http://www.facebook.com/Civitas-Press

www.ingramcontent.com/pod-product-compliance
Lightning Source LLC
LaVergne TN
LVHW050630100826
845148LV00011B/1819

* 9 7 8 0 6 1 5 8 9 6 5 4 0 *